'BENEDICTUS'
'MALEDICTUS'

The Discourse of the Other and the Emergence of the Subject of the Unconscious

Elizeu Antônio de Assis

Associação Brasileira de Psicanálise - ABraPsi

ISBN 13 nº 978-65-989847-2-4
ISBN 10 nº 65-989847-2-6
DOI 10.5281/zenodo.17814822
DOI - 10.29327/5736959

Cover design by: Assis, Elizeu
Library of Congress Control Number: LCCN - 2025926073
Printed in the United States of America

PREFACE

The Brazilian Psychoanalysis Association (ABraPsi) is pleased to present the work "Benedictus" "Maledictus": The Discourse of the Other and the Emergence of the Subject of the Unconscious, a study that deepens the complex relationship between word, desire, and subjectivity in the psychoanalytic tradition.

Psychologist and psychoanalyst Elizeu Antônio de Assis brings to this work a singular trajectory, which articulates scientific rigor, interdisciplinary, and an ethical commitment to listening to the subject of the unconscious. His training as a Master in Communication, Information and Health Sciences from Fiocruz and a Ph.D. in History from UFOP confers upon his psychoanalytic reflection a rare theoretical depth, as well as an acute sensitivity to the complex mediations between subjectivity, language, and culture.

The author proposes a fundamental reflection on

the word as a paradoxical territory—both redeeming and condemning—and on how social discourse, the Discourse of the Other, attempts to capture the subject in formulas and diagnoses. However, it is in the breach of this discourse that the subject of the unconscious can emerge, affirming its desire and instating a new ethics of the word.

With a rigorous foundation in Freudian and Lacanian theory, this work traverses the path from the alienated word to the full word, exploring how the clinic can transform the symptom (maledictum) into signification and act (benedictum). Each chapter constitutes a necessary moment in this crossing, offering the reader not only concepts but a thinking experience that reflects the analytical work itself.

For ABraPsi, this work symbolizes the commitment to a living psychoanalysis, which is not content with dogmatic repetition but dares the creative elaboration of its own theoretical field. It constitutes, therefore, mandatory reading for psychoanalysts, scholars, and all those interested in the destinies of the subject in the contemporary world.

Brazilian Psychoanalysis Association (ABraPsi)

A Reference in Psychoanalytic Research and Training and social commitment.

A JOURNEY THROUGH THE WORD
THAT ALIENATES AND LIBERATES

In this fundamental work, the reader is invited to traverse the paths of the word in its dual face: that which captures the subject in the signifiers of the Other (Maledictus) and that which, resignified, becomes an instrument of liberation and self-invention (Benedictus).

Through a rigorous investigation that articulates Freud and Lacan, the book unveils how the same word that constitutes us in alienation can become a vehicle for subjective emancipation. From the capture mechanisms of the Discourse of the Master to the ethics of the Discourse of the Analyst, from the petrified word of the symptom to the creative act of the subject, this work offers a theoretical compass to navigate the complex territories of psychoanalytic clinic.

Ideal for psychoanalysts in training, experienced professionals, and scholars of the humanities, *"Benedictus"*

"*Maledictus*" represents an essential contribution to understanding the destinies of the contemporary subject and the ethical possibilities of its emergence in the face of the determinations of discourse.

A work that transforms our understanding of the therapeutic power of the word and its radical limits.

I WANT TO TAKE MY STREET
BAND TO THE STREET

Song by Sérgio Sampaio · 1973 - (Free translation)

There are those who say I wore a nightcap to sleep
That I lost my mouth, that I fled the fight
That I fell from the branch and saw no way out
That I died of fear when the stick broke

There are those who say I know nothing
That I am nothing and don't apologize
That I am not to blame, but that I was careless
And that Durango Kid almost caught me

I want to take my street band to the street
To play, to make it moan
I want to take my street band to the street
To sway, to give and sell

Me, I wanted this and that
Another kilo of that, one less cricket in this
This is what I need or it's none of this
I want everyone in this carnival

I want to take my street band to the street
To play, to make it moan
I want to take my street band to the street
To sway, to give and sell

SAMPAIO, Sérgio. *I want to take my street band to the street.* Rio de Janeiro: CBS, 1973.

CATALOGING RECORD

Dados Internacionais de Catalogação na Publicação (CIP)
(Câmara Brasileira do Livro, SP, Brasil)

```
Assis, Elizeu Antônio de
   'Benedictus' 'Maledictus' : the discourse of
the other and the emergence of the subject of the
unconscious / Elizeu Antônio de Assis ; tradução
Fatima Aparecida de Assis. -- João Monlevade, MG :
Associação Brasileira de Psicanálise - ABraPsi,
2026.

   Título original: Benedictus Maledictus
   ISBN 978-65-989847-2-4

   1. Comportamento - Análise 2. Comportamento -
Aspectos psicológicos 3. Doenças mentais 4. Emoções
5. Neurodiversidade 6. Psicanálise 7. Psicologia
8. Saúde mental I. Assis, Fatima Aparecida de.
II. Título.

25-321422.0                                  CDD-150
```

Índices para catálogo sistemático:

1. Comportamento : Análise : Psicanálise   150

Henrique Ribeiro Soares - Bibliotecário - CRB-8/9314

PALAVRAS CHAVE:

1. Human behavior – Analysis
2. Human behavior - Psychological aspects
3. Emotions - Psychological aspects
4. Neurodiversity
5. Pathology
6. Psychoanalysis - Psychological aspects
7. Mental health
8. Disorders
9. Mental disorders
10. Psychology
11. Psychoanalysis
12. Psychoanalytic treatment

INTRODUCTION

The title of this book, *'Benedictus' 'Maledictus': The Discourse of the Other and the Emergence of the Subject of the Unconscious*, is not a mere figure of speech but the central thesis we propose on the word in psychoanalysis. The word is, at the same time, the instrument of our salvation and the mark of our condemnation. It is Benedicta for being the only means through which the subject can constitute itself, symbolize the world, and, in the clinic, reach the truth of its desire. But it is Maledicta for being the entry point of alienation, of the imposition of the Other, and of the petrification of the symptom.

This duality manifests itself in the fundamental tension that structures psychic life: the struggle between the Discourse of the Other—which here presents itself as the Discourse About the subject—and the Emergence of the Subject of the Unconscious. The Discourse of the Other is the narrative imposed upon us, the social judgment, the established knowledge that attempts to reduce the complexity of the subject to a formula, a category, a diagnosis. It is the voice that, in Sérgio Sampaio's song (1973), proclaims: *"There are those who say I wore a nightcap to sleep, that I lost my mouth, that I fled the fight"*. It is the discourse that defines us from a lack, a flaw, a passivity, positioning us as Maledictus.

However, the subject is not reducible to this condemnation. In a moment of rupture, the same song erupts with the voice of desire: *"I want to take my street band to the street"*. This is the inflection point that interests us: the Emergence of the Subject of the Unconscious. It is the moment when the subject, tired of being "spoken" by the Other, assumes the full word, the word that does not apologize but launches itself into the world as an act. It is the passage from *"There are those who say"* to *"Me, I wanted this and that"*, an ethical movement of separation and assumption of one's own lack and desire. It is the word that becomes Benedicta for the subject.

Psychoanalysis, from Freud and, more radically with Lacan, is the field where this struggle unfolds. It is in Free Association that the Maledicta word of the symptom—

the signifier that binds and condemns—can be resignified and transformed into the Benedicta word of interpretation and subjective truth. This book proposes a journey to unravel this dynamic, starting from the Discourse of the Other—source of alienating blessings and curses—to the Emergence of the Subject of the Unconscious—a moment of rescue and affirmation of one's own word.

We will begin with the Inaugural Word and alienation in the Discourse of the Other, passing through the symbolic function (Benedicta) and the failure of the Real (Maledicta). We will dedicate specific chapters to deepen the Discourse About (the Discourse of the Master) and the Discourse of the Subject (the emergence of unconscious truth). The progression will culminate in the analysis of the Act of the Word as a change of position, exploring how the body, time, and transference are traversed by this dialectic. The final objective is to demonstrate that the ethics of psychoanalysis resides in the Ethical Imperative to affirm one's own desire, subverting the discourse that imprisons us and inventing a new word for oneself.

CHAPTER 1: THE INAUGURAL WORD

*The Captured Subject: Alienation
in the Discourse of the Other*

1.1 The Word as Raw Material: From Freud to Lacan

Psychoanalysis, since its beginnings with Sigmund Freud, established itself as a practice founded on the cure through speech. The genesis of the psychoanalytic method is intrinsically linked to the discovery that the word, in its dimension of report and free association, possesses a singular therapeutic power. The case of Anna O., treated by Josef Breuer, and the description of the cathartic method as "talking cure," demonstrate that the essential raw material of the clinic is not the biological body, but the subject constituted in and by language. The word, therefore, is not just a vehicle for communicating psychic contents; it is the very medium where the unconscious manifests and structures itself. Freud, describing the analytical work, emphasizes that the symptom is a symbolic formation, and that the cure operates through the word: "Hysterics suffer mainly from reminiscences" (FREUD; BREUER, 1895, p. 12). The word, when articulated, allows the discharge of the affect until then retained.

In Freud, the primacy of the word is established through the distinction between thing-representation (Sachvorstellung) and word-representation (Wortvorstellung). The Freudian unconscious, although conceived as a reservoir of drives, is accessible through elements linked to language. Repression, the central mechanism of neurosis, acts on representations, preventing their access to consciousness. The analytical work consists, thus, in undoing this repression, allowing the repressed thing-representations to find their link with word-representations. The symptom, from this perspective, is a symbolic substitute for an unspoken word, an enigma to be deciphered. Freud (1915, p. 180) clarifies that "the unconscious representation is, therefore, the thing-representation, without the corresponding word-representation." Analysis aims precisely to reestablish this link.

However, the Freudian unconscious is not entirely

linguistic. The concept of ideational representative (Vorstellungsrepräsentanz) designates the raw material of the unconscious, something on the frontier between the drive-based and the representational. It is this concept that Jacques Lacan will rescue and reinterpret, elevating the word and language to a founding status for psychoanalysis. Lacan, proposing that "the unconscious is structured like a language," performs an epistemological turn that redefines analytic practice, situating it in the field of linguistics and philosophy of language. Lacan not only recognizes the importance of the word but elevates it to the condition of cause of the subject. The unconscious, for Lacan, is a system of signifiers that operates according to the laws of language—metaphor and metonymy. In *The Function and Field of Speech and Language in Psychoanalysis*, Lacan (1998, p. 248) states that "the unconscious is the discourse of the Other." This statement is central to understanding the primordial alienation of the subject.

Metaphor, for Lacan, corresponds to the Freudian mechanism of condensation, where one signifier substitutes another, creating new meaning and producing the symptom. Metonymy, in turn, corresponds to displacement, where meaning slides incessantly in the signifying chain, manifesting a desire that can never be named directly. The word, in its Lacanian dimension as signifier, is the discrete and differential element that composes the structure of the unconscious. The signifier does not represent a thing, but represents the subject for another signifier. This definition implies that the subject does not preexist language but is produced by it. The word, therefore, is the raw material not only of the clinic but of subjectivity itself. The transition from Freud to Lacan marks the passage from a psychoanalysis that uses the word to a psychoanalysis founded on the structure of language, where the unconscious reveals itself as a discourse of the Other.

1.2 The Function of Speech and Language in the Constitution of the Subject

The Lacanian distinction between language (langage) and speech (parole) is fundamental to understanding the process of the subject's constitution. Language is the symbolic structure, the system of signifiers that preexists the subject and determines it. It is the treasure of signifiers, the set of rules that make communication possible and, primordially, the existence of the unconscious. Language is the field of the Other (A), the instance in which the subject must inscribe itself to become humanized.

Speech, on the other hand, is the singular act of appropriation of this structure by the subject. It is the contingent and particular use of language. It is in speech that the subject manifests itself, but also where it hides. Lacan, in *The Function and Field of Speech and Language in Psychoanalysis*, argues that speech has two essential dimensions: empty speech and full speech. Full speech is defined as that which "constitutes the truth of the subject" (LACAN, 1998, p. 256), in contrast to empty speech, which exhausts itself on the surface of discourse.

Empty speech is the discourse that unfolds on the surface, that does not engage the subject in its truth. It is the speech that repeats clichés, gets lost in generalities, serving to maintain the illusion of a cohesive ego and transparent communication. It is the discourse of the ego, of consciousness, which moves away from unconscious desire.

Full speech, in contrast, is that which, when uttered, transforms the subject. It is the speech that touches the point of truth of desire, that reveals the crack of the unconscious. Full speech is not that which recounts a fact with accuracy, but that which engages the subject in its singular history. It is the speech that, when articulated, resignifies the past and projects the future. The goal of analysis, according to Lacan, is the passage from empty speech to full speech, allowing the subject to appropriate its history and desire.

The constitution of the subject is, therefore, a process of entry into the field of language. The *infans*, at birth, is a being of pure need, but its appeal can only be articulated through the Other, bearer of language. The baby's cry, when interpreted by the mother (the first Other), transforms into demand. It is in this process that need alienates itself in language. The subject learns that, to be recognized and have its needs met, it must submit to the symbolic order, to the law of the signifier.

The function of speech, in this context, is that of

interpellation and recognition. By speaking, the subject seeks to be recognized by the Other. However, what it finds is the structure of language, which divides it. The speaking subject is always a divided subject ($), for it is an effect of language but can never be totally represented by it. Language, while constituting it, alienates it from a supposed imaginary plenitude.

1.3 The Discourse of the Other (Big Other) and the Imposition of Social Narrative

The concept of the Other (A, capitalized) is a pillar of Lacanian theory and fundamental to understanding the initial capture of the subject. The Other is not a specific person, but the place of language, the treasure of the signifier, the repository of law and culture. It is the place where the subject seeks recognition and from where its identity emanates.

The Discourse of the Other is, therefore, the set of signifiers, rules, values, and expectations that preexist the subject and shape it. It is the social, familial, and cultural narrative imposed on the individual since birth. The subject is, initially, an object of the Other's desire. The child is interpellated by the Other through questions like: "What do you want to be?", "What are you to me?". The answer to these interpellations is given by the Other, even before the subject can articulate its own answer.

The imposition of the social narrative occurs through language. The Other names the subject, classifies it, inserts it into a genealogy and a network of relations. The proper name, for example, is the first signifier that marks the subject, inserting it into the symbolic order. Before being "I," the subject is "son/daughter of," "member of," "bearer of a name." This naming is the first act of capture, for the subject is forced to identify with the signifiers the Other offers it.

The Discourse of the Other is what we call the Discourse About the subject. It is the discourse that attempts to fix meaning, that seeks a coherent and stable identity for the individual. It is the discourse that affirms: "You are like this," "You must do this," "You are not capable of that." It is the discourse that, metaphorically, in the cited song, says: "There are those who say I wore a nightcap to sleep, that I lost my mouth..." This discourse is the source of alienation, for it offers the subject an imaginary identity (the ego), but distances it from its unconscious truth (the subject).

Law, morality, religion, science, and, paradoxically, certain strands of psychoanalysis (those Lacan criticized as "ego psychology") operate under the Discourse of the Other. They seek total knowledge about the subject, trying to eliminate its division and desire. The Discourse of the Other is, in essence, the Discourse of the Master, which attempts to reduce the subject to an object susceptible to domination and knowledge.

The function of the Other, however, is paradoxical. Although it is the place of alienation, it is also the place from which full speech can emerge. The Other is incomplete (A barred). The treasure of the signifier possesses holes, failures, which prevent the Discourse of the Other from being totalizing. It is the incompleteness of the Other that enables the emergence of the subject's desire. The imposition of the social narrative is the condition for subjectivation, but liberation from this narrative is the goal of analysis.

1.4 The Initial Position of Alienation and Capture by the Discourse of the Other

The constitution of the subject, according to Lacan, is marked by two logical operations: alienation and separation. This chapter focuses on the first, alienation, which is the initial and necessary position of the subject in the field of the Other.

Alienation is the operation by which the subject constitutes itself in the field of the Other. Lacan illustrates it with the dilemma of the forced choice: "Your money or your life." If the subject chooses life, it loses the money; if it chooses the money, it loses life. In alienation, the choice is always exclusive and entails a loss. In the context of language, the subject is forced to choose between being and meaning. According to Lacan (1988, p. 200), alienation is the "union of two terms which, by their conjunction, nonetheless remain exclusive." The subject, by submitting to the signifier, loses a part of its being.

If the subject chooses meaning (the discourse of the Other, the offered identity), it gains a place in the world, a name, a narrative, but loses its singular being, its desire. It becomes an echo of the Other, a captured subject. If it chooses being (its desire, the unsayable), it loses meaning, social recognition, risking silence and psychosis.

Alienation is, therefore, the capture of the subject by the signifier. The subject is forced to identify with the signifiers of the Other, to submit to the law of language. This submission is what makes it a speaking subject, but also what divides it. The alienated subject is one who speaks but does not hear itself, who repeats the discourse of the Other without knowing what it truly desires.

The capture by the Discourse of the Other manifests itself in the clinic through empty speech. The alienated patient is one who recounts its history in a coherent manner, but without passion, without gaps, without slips. It repeats the narrative it was taught, the narrative the Other imposed on it. The analyst's work, at this moment, is to destabilize this narrative, to introduce the crack, the cut, that will allow the subject to initiate the movement of exiting alienation.

Alienation is a necessary condition for subjectivation. There is no subject outside of language. However, it is not a sufficient condition. The subject needs to transit from alienation to separation, the theme of subsequent chapters. Separation is the operation by which the subject detaches itself from the Other, discovering that the Other is incomplete and that its desire does not coincide with the desire of the Other.

Chapter 1, by focusing on alienation, establishes the starting point of the book: the subject in its position of capture, under the yoke of the Discourse About. It is from this submission to the Maledicta word of the Other that the path to the Benedicta word of the Affirmation of the Subject can be traced. Understanding alienation is the key to understanding the urgency of the act of "taking the street band to the street," a metaphor for the movement of separation and assumption of desire.

1.5 The Depth of Alienation: The Concept of

Vorstellungsrepräsentanz and the Master Signifier

To deepen the understanding of alienation and capture by the Discourse of the Other, it is crucial to return to the conceptual transition between Freud and Lacan, specifically regarding the raw material of the unconscious. Freud, as mentioned, used the term *Vorstellungsrepräsentanz* (ideational representative) to designate the repressed psychic element that serves as a link between the drive and the symbolic register. This representative is not the drive itself, nor the conscious representation, but what represents the drive in the psyche. Repression acts upon this representative, preventing its link with consciousness.

Lacan, rereading Freud in light of structural linguistics, translates and transforms this concept into the signifier. The raw material of the unconscious becomes the signifier, the differential element that, by its nature, is devoid of meaning in itself but acquires value by its position in the chain. The unconscious, structured like a language, is a system of articulated signifiers.

Alienation occurs precisely because the subject, upon entering language, is forced to identify with a signifier that represents it in the field of the Other. This is the Master Signifier (S1). The S1 is the signifier that attempts to confer a fixed identity upon the subject ("You are the son/daughter," "You are the intelligent one," "You are the problem"). It is the signifier emanating from the Other that captures the being of the subject.

The capture is alienating because the signifier, by definition, cannot represent the subject in its totality. The signifier represents the subject for another signifier (S2), and so on, in an infinite chain. The subject ($) is what is between the signifiers, what escapes representation. Alienation is the illusion that the subject is its S1, that it is the narrative the Other imposed upon it.

The clinic of alienation is the clinic of repetition. The alienated subject repeats its S1, its Master Signifier, in all its relations and throughout its discourse. It lives under the yoke of the Discourse About, which condemns it to be what the Other said it was. The word, in this context, is **Maledicta**, for it is the instrument of its imprisonment.

1.6 The Dialectic of Demand and Desire in Alienation

The alienation of the subject in language is mediated by demand. The baby, by crying, expresses a need (hunger, cold, pain). However, the mother (the first Other) does not respond only to the need; she responds with language. The cry is interpreted as a demand for love and presence.

Demand, for Lacan, is the need that passes through the filter of the signifier. When articulated, the need alienates itself in language and transforms into something more: a demand for unconditional love. The subject demands the object that will satisfy its need, but, fundamentally, it demands recognition from the Other.

The problem of alienation lies in the fact that the Other, being incomplete, can never totally satisfy the demand for love. What the Other offers is always a substitute, a partial object. It is in this gap between demand and satisfaction that desire arises. Desire is what remains when the need is satisfied and the demand for love is frustrated.

The alienated subject is one that remains trapped in demand. It continues to demand from the Other what the Other cannot give (the object that would complete it). The Discourse About the subject is the discourse that keeps it in this position of demand, promising a satisfaction that never realizes. The social narrative imposes that the subject must demand success, wealth, beauty, and that satisfying these demands will complete it.

Alienation is the refusal to recognize desire as that which is irreducible and cannot be satisfied by demand. Desire is what moves the subject out of the field of the Other, in search of its own word. The capture by the Discourse of the Other is the persistence in the illusion that happiness resides in the satisfaction of demand.

Psychoanalysis, by working with speech, aims precisely to detach the subject from demand and confront it with the structure of its desire. The passage from alienation to separation is the passage from demand to desire, from the discourse of the Other to the Affirmation of the Subject.

1.7 Empty Speech as Expression of Alienation

The distinction between empty speech and full speech is the clinical indicator of alienation. Empty speech is the discourse of the subject trapped in the Discourse of the Other. It is the speech that has no weight, that does not engage the subject in its truth.

Empty speech is characterized by repetition. The subject repeats the story it was told, the signifiers the Other imposed on it. It speaks *about* itself, but not *from* itself. It is the discourse of the ego (imaginary), which presents itself as coherent and unified, but which hides the division of the subject ($).

In the clinic, empty speech manifests as:

1. **Generalities and Clichés:** The patient uses ready-made phrases, moral maxims, or rational explanations that do not touch its singular suffering.
2. **Historical Discourse:** The patient reports facts and

events in a chronological and linear manner, without resignification or accompanying affect. The history is told but not assumed.

3. **Identification with the Symptom:** The patient identifies with its symptom ("I am a depressive," "I am an anxious person"), transforming it into its Master Signifier (S1), which imprisons it even more in the Discourse About.

Empty speech is the symptom of alienation, for it demonstrates that the subject speaks from the place of the Other. It repeats what the Other said about it. The analyst's work, at this point, is to cut this repetition, to introduce silence, punctuation, which forces the subject to go beyond what is being said.

Full speech, which will be the focus of later chapters, is the opposite of empty speech. It is the word that, when said, creates the subject. It is the word that reveals desire, that touches the point of truth of the unconscious. The passage from empty speech to full speech is the very crossing from alienation to separation.

1.8 The Paradox of the Inaugural Word

Chapter 1, titled The Inaugural Word, points to the central paradox of psychoanalysis. The word is inaugural because it is what inaugurates the subject in the field of language. Without the word, there is no human subject. However, this inauguration is, simultaneously, a capture. The word that confers being upon us is the same that alienates us.

The inaugural word is the word of the Other, the first signifier that marks us. It is the word that inserts us into the symbolic order, but that condemns us to be represented by something that never represents us totally. It is the word that makes us subjects, but that divides us.

The book, by starting with alienation, establishes the starting point for the subject's journey. Psychoanalysis is the path of return, the attempt to dealienate the word, to transform it from **Maledicta** to **Benedicta**. It is the search for the word that, instead of repeating the Discourse About, affirms the singular desire of the subject.

Understanding alienation is the first step towards the Affirmation of the Subject. The subject can only separate from the Other if it recognizes how much it is bound to it. Chapter 1, therefore, serves as the diagnosis of the human condition in language: the condition of being a captured subject, but with the possibility of, through speech, finding the crack for its freedom.

1.9 The Structure of the Unconscious and Linguistic Alienation

To consolidate the idea that the word is the raw material of psychoanalysis and the cause of alienation, it is fundamental to detail the structure of the Lacanian unconscious. The statement that "the unconscious is structured like a language" implies that it is not a chaotic or pre-verbal domain, but a system governed by the laws of the signifier.

The unconscious is the discourse of the Other. It is composed of the signifiers the subject received and that constituted it, but which were not integrated into its consciousness. Linguistic alienation occurs because the subject is spoken by this discourse before it can speak. The laws governing the unconscious are the same as those governing language: metaphor and metonymy.

Metaphor (condensation) is the mechanism that produces the symptom. The symptom is a signifier that substitutes another repressed signifier. For example, a phobia is a signifier (the phobic object) that substitutes the signifier of the desire of the Other. The subject alienates itself in the symptom, identifying with the metaphor that imprisons it.

Metonymy (displacement) is the mechanism that manifests desire. Desire is what slides in the signifying chain, from one signifier to another. The subject, when speaking, never says its desire directly, but manifests it in the displacement of its discourse. Metonymic alienation is the incessant search for an object that satisfies desire, a search always frustrated, for desire is the lack itself.

Alienation is the condition of being a divided subject ($). The subject is divided between its ego (imaginary, coherent) and its being (unconscious, fragmented). The inaugural word, by inserting it into language, divides it. It is the effect of language, but can never be totally represented by it. Alienation is the illusion that this division can be sutured, that the subject can become a complete ego.

The Discourse of the Other, by imposing its narrative,

attempts to suture this division, offering the subject an S1 (Master Signifier) that defines it. Capture is the acceptance of this suture, the persistence in the empty word that repeats the S1. Chapter 1, by detailing this structure, prepares the ground for understanding separation, which is the refusal of this suture and the acceptance of division.

1.10 Lacan's Critique of Ego Psychology and the Reaffirmation of the Word

The emphasis on the word as raw material and on alienation as the initial condition of the subject is the core of Lacan's critique of Ego Psychology (*Ego Psychology*), which dominated American psychoanalysis in the post-war period. Lacan accused this current of having betrayed the Freudian discovery of the unconscious by attempting to strengthen the ego (the conscious self) and adapt it to social reality.

For Lacan, the ego is an imaginary formation, an illusion of coherence and unity that represents the point of greatest alienation of the subject. The ego is what identifies with the Discourse of the Other, with the social narrative. Strengthening the ego is, for Lacan, strengthening alienation.

Lacan's reaffirmation of the word is an attempt to return psychoanalysis to its original field: the field of language and the unconscious. The cure is not in the adaptation of the ego to reality, but in the passage from empty speech to full speech, in the confrontation of the subject with the truth of its desire.

The word, therefore, is the instrument of alienation, but also the instrument of liberation. It is the word that imprisons us in the Discourse About, but it is the word that, when spoken in analysis, allows us to affirm our desire and initiate the movement of separation. Chapter 1, by establishing alienation as the starting point, justifies the need for the psychoanalytic clinic as the only place where the word can be dealienated.

The Inaugural Word is, thus, the word that constitutes and captures us. The rest of the book will explore the journey to transform this inaugural word into a Final Word, a word that, instead of repeating the Other, affirms the subject in its singularity.

1.11 The Legacy of Saussure and the Arbitrariness of the Signifier

For linguistic alienation to be fully understood, it is crucial to revisit the legacy of Ferdinand de Saussure, whose structural linguistics served as the basis for Lacanian theory. Saussure established that the linguistic sign is composed of two faces: the signifier (the acoustic image) and the signified (the concept). The relationship between them is arbitrary, meaning there is no natural link between the word "tree" and the concept of a tree. Saussure (2006, p. 81) states that "the bond between the signifier and the signified is arbitrary." This arbitrariness is what allows Lacan to displace the signifier into the field of the unconscious, where it operates autonomously.

Lacan radicalizes this arbitrariness. For him, the signifier is not linked to a fixed signified, but to other signifiers. The signifier acquires value through its difference from others in the chain. It is this arbitrariness and this differential nature that make language a system of pure alterity, a system that preexists and dominates the subject.

Alienation occurs because the subject is forced to insert itself into this arbitrary system. It does not choose the signifiers that constitute it; it receives them from the Other. The inaugural word is, therefore, an arbitrary signifier that the Other imposes upon it. The subject is captured by a network of signifiers that have no inherent meaning but, together, form the Discourse About that defines it.

The capture is so profound that the subject forgets the arbitrariness. It comes to believe that its S1 (Master Signifier) is its essence, that the word that defines it is its truth. Analysis, by working with speech, aims to denaturalize this belief, showing that the S1 is just a signifier, an arbitrary element in the chain, and that the subject is what is between the signifiers, what escapes its representation.

Alienation is the illusion that the word is transparent, that it says what is. Psychoanalysis, on the contrary, reveals that the word is opaque, that it hides more than it reveals, and that the subject is the effect of this opacity. Chapter 1, by detailing linguistic alienation, prepares the reader for the complexity of full speech, which will be the attempt to use the opacity of language to reveal the truth of desire.

1.12 The Alienated Condition and the Necessary Crossing

Chapter 1 established the initial condition of the subject in psychoanalysis: alienation in the field of language, under the yoke of the Discourse of the Other. The word, in its inaugural dimension, is the cause of this capture, being simultaneously Benedicta (for constituting the subject) and Maledicta (for imprisoning it).

The central thesis demonstrated that the subject is, initially, a captured subject, living under the Discourse About that defines and limits it. The word it uses is, largely, an empty word, a repetition of the signifiers of the Other.

The next chapters will explore the possibility of crossing this alienation. If this chapter diagnosed the capture, the subsequent chapters will be the therapeutics of separation and the Affirmation of the Subject. The book's journey is the passage from the Maledicta word of the Discourse About to the Benedicta word of the Discourse of the Subject, culminating in the ethical act of affirming one's own desire.

Understanding alienation is the starting point for the clinic. The analyst, listening to the patient's empty word, seeks the point of fissure, the slip, the joke, where the subject of the unconscious ($) can emerge. Chapter 1, by detailing the structure of alienation, justifies the need for psychoanalysis as the only practice that bets on the word as a path to subjective freedom.

The reader is invited to follow the progression, understanding that the Affirmation of the Subject is not the negation of alienation, but its crossing, the acceptance of division and the invention of a word that is, finally, its own.

References

- FREUD, S. (1915). The unconscious. In: Standard Edition of the Complete Psychological Works of Sigmund Freud. London: Hogarth Press, 1996. v. XIV.

- FREUD, S.; BREUER, J. (1895). Studies on hysteria. In: Standard Edition of the Complete Psychological Works of Sigmund Freud. London: Hogarth Press, 1996. v. II.

- LACAN, J. (1953). The Function and Field of Speech and Language in Psychoanalysis. In: Écrits. New York: W.W. Norton & Company, 2006.

- LACAN, J. (1964). The Seminar, Book XI: The Four Fundamental Concepts of Psychoanalysis. New York: W.W. Norton & Company, 1998.

- SAUSSURE, F. de. (1916). Course in General Linguistics. New York: McGraw-Hill, 2011.

- CASTRO, J. C. L. de. The unconscious as language: from Freud to Lacan. Casa, v. 3, n. 1, 2009.

- ZANOLA, P. C. Alienation and separation in Lacan's Seminar 11. Tempo Psicanalítico, v. 51, n. 2, 2019.

CHAPTER 2: BENEDICTUS: THE SYMBOLIC FUNCTION AND THE PROMISE OF CURE

The Power to Name and the Emergence of the Subject

If the previous chapter diagnosed the alienated condition of the subject—captured by the Discourse of the Other and condemned to the repetition of empty speech—this chapter advances towards its necessary dialectical antithesis. Starting from the need for crossing established in the previous Chapter, we will now explore how the same word that alienates can become an instrument of liberation.

Benedictus designates here the redemptive power of the word, its face of Symbolic Function that, far from merely capturing, promotes the emergence of the subject of the unconscious. This is the central dialectic that moves the psychoanalytic clinic: the same word that alienates (Maledicta) is the one that, resignified, liberates

(Benedicta). Psychoanalysis operates precisely in this transition, betting on the capacity of language to subvert the petrification of the symptom.

Understanding the Symbolic Function requires mapping the three Lacanian registers—the Real, the Imaginary, and the Symbolic—the latter being the domain of Law and language which, while dividing, constitutes the subject as parlêtre. The word, in this register, is not a means, but the very condition of possibility of the subject.

The Symbolic Function is, therefore, the axis that enables the crossing from alienation to separation, from the Discourse of the Other to the Affirmation of the Subject. The word is Benedicta because it is the only instrument capable of operating this cure: the invention of the self from the assumption of one's own lack and desire.

2.1 The Word as Foundational Act: From Alienation to Symbolization

The condition of the **Maledictus**, as demonstrated,

is that of a subject captured by the Master Signifier (S1) of the Other, condemned to the repetition of empty speech. The passage to the position of **Benedictus** occurs through the foundational act of **symbolization**. In Lacan, symbolization is not a passive attribution of meanings, but an act that actively structures psychic reality and institutes the social bond (LACAN, 1998).

While in the Imaginary register the subject confuses itself with the desire of the Other, the symbolic word introduces difference and lack. It names, distinguishes, and, in doing so, creates a space of separation between the subject and the object of its desire. The word, as a signifier, denaturalizes the world, transforming brute Real into a human reality, mediated by language. The Symbolic Function instates the signifying chain in which the unconscious is structured.

The subject is an effect of this chain, and its truth is dispersed there. Symbolization is, therefore, the process of inscription into this chain and acceptance of the Law that governs it—the Law of language, of difference, and of prohibition. It is the articulated word that allows the circulation of desire and the possibility of narrating a history. Symbolization is the condition of possibility for the historicization of the subject, for it confers meaning and temporality to events (FRANÇÓIA, 2007). The word, when used to name the lack, transforms itself into the vector of separation that overcomes alienation. The subject of the **Maledictus** is one who cannot symbolize its lack, remaining trapped in the demand of the Other.

2.1.1 The Symbolic, the Imaginary, and the Real: The Structural Triad

To understand the operation of **Benedictus**, it is fundamental to situate the Symbolic Function in the Lacanian triad (R.I.S.), the structure that sustains psychic reality.

1. **The Imaginary:** Register of the image, identification, and the dual relationship. Field of the illusion of completeness, where the word is empty, repeating clichés and the desire of the Other.

2. **The Real:** What is irreducible to symbolization. The traumatic, the impossible to say, which insists and returns. It is the object *a* as an unavoidable remainder.

3. **The Symbolic:** Register of language, Law, and structure. Field of the Other (A), treasure of the signifier. Where the word becomes **Benedicta**, that is, full, articulator of

desire and history.

The Symbolic Function is what allows the tying together of these three registers. The word, by naming, introduces lack into the Imaginary and encircles the Real, mitigating its overwhelming return. The cure, in this sense, is the strengthening of the Symbolic, the capacity of the subject to use the **Benedicta** word to mediate its relationship with the Imaginary and the Real. It is the only element capable of operating this tying, conferring structure to the chaos of the drives.

2.1.2 The Word and the Constitution of the Object a

Symbolization is intrinsically linked to the constitution of the object *a*, the cause of desire. The object *a* is not the object of need, but the remainder lost upon the subject's entry into language.

When the subject demands from the Other, its need alienates itself in the signifier. The Other, being incomplete, never totally satisfies this demand. The residue of this dissatisfaction is the object *a*. The word, by naming the demand, creates the gap where the object *a* installs itself. Thus, the **Benedicta** word is, paradoxically, what creates the lost object and, with it, desire—the very condition of being a subject. Without the word, the subject would remain fixated on pure need. Symbolization is, therefore, the passage from need to demand and from demand to desire. "Desire is the metonymy of the lack-in-being" (LACAN, 1998, p. 518).

The word, by articulating desire, inscribes it in the signifying chain, allowing its circulation. Psychoanalytic cure includes the capacity of the subject to recognize the object *a* as the cause of its desire and to take responsibility for it. Lacan's celebrated formula—"The symbol manifests itself first of all as the murder of the thing, and this death constitutes in the subject the eternalization of its desire" (1998, p. 269)—condenses this operation of **Benedictus**. By naming the "thing" (the *das Ding* of Freud), the word kills it in its real presence, transforming it into a signifier. It is this "death" that, by eternalizing desire in the metonymic search, frees the subject from the tyranny of the Real and inserts it into the order of culture and Law.

2.2 The Name-of-the-Father and the Inscription of Law in the Symbolic Order

The signifier that operates the definitive insertion of the subject into the Symbolic Order and consolidates the position of **Benedictus** is the **Name-of-the-Father**. This concept does not refer to the person of the father, but to a function, a signifier that represents Law and prohibition (ZENONI, 2007).

The paternal function sustains the Symbolic Function, regulating the relationship with the primordial Other. The Name-of-the-Father is the signifier that interposes itself between the child and the mother's desire, barring the imaginary fusion and instating symbolic castration—which is the acceptance of lack and the renunciation of completeness. The power to name, inherent to **Benedictus**, is the power to institute a world for the subject. The Name-of-the-Father, by prohibiting (incest, for example), promises: it opens the field of culture and the Other as a space for the circulation of desire. The word, as Law, is what allows the constitution of the social bond.

The failure in the inscription of the Name-of-the-Father—**foreclosure**—is, for Lacan, the structural condition of psychosis (LUSTOZA, 2018). In this case, the signifier of the Law is not symbolized, the Symbolic Function does not consolidate, and the Real returns in an overwhelming form, as hallucinations and delusions. Foreclosure demonstrates, by negative means, the structuring power of the **Benedicta** word. Where it fails, the chaos of the Real erupts. The inscription of the Name-of-the-Father allows the **Paternal Metaphor**, the operation that substitutes the Desire of the Mother with the Name-of-the-Father, conferring upon the subject a place in the genealogical chain and social structure. The word, here, is **Benedicta** for being the vehicle for transmitting the Law that humanizes and enables desire.

2.3 Symbolization and the Promise of Cure: The Full Word

The promise of cure in psychoanalysis, the core of its ethics, resides in the possibility of the subject transforming the empty word of the **Maledictus** into the **full word** (*parole* *pleine*) of the **Benedictus**. The full word is the act of speech that engages the subject in its truth, reveals the crack of the unconscious, and resignifies its history.

The Lacanian cure is not the elimination of the symptom, but a change of subjective position: the passage from being spoken by the Other to speaking of oneself, assuming one's own desire. The full word is the vehicle of this assumption. "The full word is that which constitutes the truth of the subject" (LACAN, 1998, p. 256). It does not tell a factual truth, but *makes* the truth of the subject emerge, creating a new sense that detaches it from the fixity of the symptom.

The therapeutic effect of symbolization is the capacity to, through the word, name and thus encircle the Real. The symptom is a failed attempt to symbolize the traumatic Real. Analysis, through free association, incites the subject to weave a signifying network around the unnamable. By naming what was unsayable, the subject integrates the traumatic into its history, transforming sterile repetition into narrative. The full word is, therefore, an ethical act of assuming responsibility for one's own desire and one's own speech. The subject who reaches the full word is not a complete subject, but one who, accepting its incompleteness (\$), invents from it a new way of being. The word is **Benedicta** because, by allowing symbolization, it opens the future, freeing the subject from the repetition of the past.

2.4 Free Association and the Ethics of Benedictus

The clinical device par excellence for the emergence of **Benedictus** is **Free Association**. The fundamental rule —"say whatever comes to mind"—is an ethical invitation to the full use of the word, without censorship. It is the invitation for the subject to launch itself into speech, in its failure and incoherence, trusting that it is in this act of saying that the **Maledicta** word of the symptom can transmute into the **Benedicta** word of truth.

By suspending censorship, Free Association allows the signifying chain of the unconscious to articulate itself freely, revealing the fissures in the Discourse of the Other. The word, in this context, becomes the vehicle of the truth of the subject. It does not know what it says, but what it says is its truth. The **Ethical Imperative** of psychoanalysis is, thus, to affirm one's own desire through the word. The act of saying is an act of courage, which confronts lack and division. The **Promise of Cure** of **Benedictus** is not happiness, but freedom: the freedom to be the subject that manifests itself in the crack of its own saying, that is not reduced to the Discourse of the Other, but that, from it, creates its own word.

2.5 Symbolic Mediation in the Emergence of the Subject

This chapter established the Symbolic Function as the antagonistic and necessary pole to the Maledictus explored previously. In it, the word revealed itself as the operator of mediation between alienation and the emergence of the subject of the unconscious.

The word demonstrated itself as the vector that, as Maledictus, inserts the subject into Law and alienation, but that, as Benedictus, liberates it through the same Law, allowing the invention of the self. The cure showed itself as the crossing from the repetition of the S1 (Master Signifier) to the articulation of desire ($) in the full word. The subject of the unconscious is one who appropriates the word to name its lack and, with this, affirms its desire.

The book's journey, which began in capture (Maledictus), found in this chapter its first liberating inflection point (Benedictus). However, this symbolic conquest reveals its own limits. The next chapter will explore precisely what in human experience resists the word and insists as a fundamental Maledictus, investigating what forms of affirmation of the subject can arise from this confrontation with the unsayable.

References

- FRANÇÓIA, Cristiane R. The Symbolic and the Psychoanalytic Clinic: The Beginning of Structuring. Adverbum, v. 2, n. 1, 2007.
- LACAN, Jacques. Écrits. New York: W.W. Norton & Company, 2006.
- LUSTOZA, Rosane Z. The formation of the concept of the Name of the Father (1938-1958). Ágora: Studies in Psychoanalytic Theory, v. 21, n. 2, p. 235-249, 2018.
- ZENONI, Alain. The course of Lacan's teaching on the question of the father. Latin American Journal of Fundamental Psychopathology, v. 10, n. 1, p. 11-23, 2007.

CHAPTER 3: MALEDICTUS: SILENCE AND THE REAL

The Symptom as Petrified Word

If symbolic mediation revealed itself as an operator of subjective transformation, demonstrating the Benedicta function of the word in the emergence of the subject, this moment of investigation returns to Maledictus to explore its intrinsic limits. Starting precisely from the constitutive limits of this symbolic mediation, we will now investigate what persists as an indomitable remainder, resistant to the signifying operation.

The journey through the word, which transited from alienation (Maledictus) to symbolic mediation (Benedictus), now confronts its point of structural impossibility. The word reveals itself as Maledicta not only for alienating, but for its radical failure to symbolize the totality of experience, leaving a residue of jouissance that insists outside the circuit of meaning.

This chapter focuses on the silence that is not peace, but the traumatic; on the symptom that does not operate as metaphor, but as petrified word; and on the performative violence of language. The central thesis maintains that the supreme curse of the word resides in the Real—that which it cannot say, what escapes the symbolic network and returns in the form of repetition, bodily suffering, and act.

Exploring this pole of Maledictus proves fundamental for the clinic, for it is in the handling of this unsayable that the possibility of a cure plays out, a cure that does not delude itself with the omnipotence of meaning but is constructed precisely in the recognition of these limits.

3.1 Lalangue and the Jouissance that Escapes Meaning

To understand the core of **Maledictus**, it is necessary to go beyond language as a pure symbolic structure and enter the Lacanian concept of **Lalangue** (*lalangue*). Lalangue is the material, pre-discursive dimension of language, the amalgam of sounds, rhythms, assonances, and equivocations that the child experiences before acquiring language as a code. It is the aspect of speech closest to the Real and the body, a vehicle of **jouissance** before being an instrument of communication (LACAN, 1985).

While symbolic language (the **Benedictus**) operates through difference and meaning, Lalangue operates through materiality and *equivocation*. It is not concerned with communicating, but with producing an effect of jouissance on the body. It manifests in involuntary puns, attraction to certain words due to their sonority, and residues of language that do not integrate into the coherent narrative of the ego. Lalangue is what, in the word, remains **Maledictum**, that is, linked to an opaque jouissance that resists signification.

3.1.1 The Materiality of the Word and its Marks on the Body

Lalangue emphasizes the *materiality* of the word, what Lacan called the *letter*. This is not the abstract signifier, but its material support inscribed on the body as a trace of jouissance. An elucidative clinical example is a patient who develops a debilitating migraine whenever, at work, he needs to "take the *head* of the project." The word "head," here, does not operate only in its metaphorical sense (leadership), but as a signifier that, through Lalangue, anchored itself in the body in a literal and painful way, producing a **Maledictum** jouissance through physical pain. The clinic, when encountering such phenomena, does not seek only to interpret the meaning, but to intervene on this material fixation, perhaps through a pun that dislodges the relationship between the word and the body.

The distinction is crucial:

Concept	Primary Register	Function	Relation with the Subject
Symbolic Language (Benedictus)	Symbolic	Communication, Meaning, Law	Allows historicization and separation ($)
Lalangue (Maledictus)	Real / Symbolic	Jouissance, Materiality, Equivocation	Binds the subject to a non-symbolized jouissance

The **jouissance** here is not pleasure, but a paradoxical satisfaction, often beyond the pleasure principle, linked to the death drive. Lalangue is the channel of this jouissance that symbolization cannot totally capture or domesticate.

It is what makes the word, even when spoken, carry with it a **Maledictum** remainder, a mark of the Real that disturbs the transparent order of meaning.

3.2 The Symptom as Petrified Word

In the **Benedictus** chapter, the symptom was approached as a metaphor to be undone. Here, under the aegis of **Maledictus**, it is apprehended in its crudeness as **petrified word**. It is the "cursed" that repeats, the truth of the subject that, unable to be articulated in the discursive chain, insists as an autistic and jouissant formation.

The symptom, in its most radical dimension, is not an error of language, but a *solution* found by the psychic apparatus to deal with an excess of jouissance or a non-symbolizable trauma. It is a truth that "becomes body," an enigmatic and fixed cipher. While the full word (**Benedictus**) liberates and historicizes, the symptomatic word (**Maledictus**) imprisons and repeats, freezing psychic time.

3.2.1 Symptomatic Satisfaction and the Death Drive

The **compulsion to repeat** (*Wiederholungszwang*) is the engine of this petrified symptom. Freud (1920) identified it as "beyond the pleasure principle": a tendency to relive painful experiences, not in search of pleasure, but as a manifestation of the death drive. Lacan rereads it as the insistence of the Real to inscribe itself. The symptom is, thus, the failed attempt—and, at the same time, the only possible one—of the subject to write, through repetitive suffering, that for which it has not found signifiers.

Let's take the case of a woman who, successively, gets involved in relationships with emotionally unavailable men, repeating a pattern she recognizes as destructive but from which she cannot free herself. This is the core of **Maledictus**: there is a jouissance in the repetition itself, a paradoxical satisfaction that sustains the symptom. She does not repeat *despite* the suffering, but *through* it. The symptom, therefore, is not only what disturbs the subject's life; it is also what sustains it in a singular manner. It offers a paradoxical satisfaction, a *jouissance* that analysis will seek not to suppress, but perhaps to dislodge and rearticulate, transforming the deadly repetition (**Maledictus**) into a repetition that can, finally, make sense for the subject (**Benedictus**).

3.3 Trauma and the Failure of Symbolization

Trauma is the paradigm of the encounter with the **Real** and, therefore, the heart of **Maledictus**. It is the event that, due to its overwhelming intensity or a lack of symbolic resources at the time, could not be inscribed in the signifying chain. Trauma is the hole in the symbolic, the active silence where the word fails.

Lacan makes a crucial distinction between the mechanisms that deal with this failure:

Mechanism	Register	Occurrence	Clinical Manifestation
Repression (*Verdrängung*)	Symbolic	The signifier is repressed into the unconscious.	Neurotic symptom (compromise formation).
Foreclosure (*Verwerfung*)	Real	The fundamental signifier (Name-of-the-Father) is not inscribed.	Psychosis (return of the foreclosed in the Real: hallucination, delusion).
Trauma	Real/Symbolic	Failure to inscribe an *event*.	Repetition, *Acting Out*, *Passage à l'Acte*, Somatization.

3.3.1 The Silence of Trauma and its Outlets: Act and Somatization

Trauma is, therefore, the point where the **Benedicta** word reveals itself impotent. What could not be said returns not as meaning, but as act (*acting out, passage à l'acte*) or as a mark on the body (somatization). *Passage à l'acte* is an abrupt exit from the symbolic scene, a fall into the Real where the subject is a pure object.

Imagine a man who, when interpellated by an authority figure echoing a paternal humiliation from childhood, reacts with an explosion of physical violence without being able to explain the reason. This is a *passage à l'acte*: the non-symbolized trauma erupts as an act, bypassing the mediation of the word completely.

Acting out, on the other hand, is an enactment, an appeal directed to the Other to give meaning to what, for the subject, remains incomprehensible. A patient who constantly puts himself in risky situations, almost asking to be saved, may be *enacting* a trauma of abandonment he cannot narrate.

Somatization, in turn, is the writing of trauma on the body itself: ulcers, chronic pain, allergies that arise in specific emotional contexts, without apparent organic cause. They are **Maledicta** words inscribed in the flesh. The curse of the word, here, is its ontological limitation. It always leaves a remainder, a residue of jouissance (the object *a*) that escapes and insists, constituting the traumatic and **Maledictum** nucleus around which the subject gravitates.

3.4 The Word as an Instrument of Violence and the Curse of the Name

The word not only fails to say the Real but can actively become an instrument of violence. This is the social and intersubjective face of **Maledictus**. Language has a **performative** dimension: it not only describes, but *does*. An insult, a humiliation, an authoritarian order are speech acts that wound, alienate, and can, in the symbolic register, "kill" the subject.

The **curse of the name** is the most insidious form of this violence. It is the word of the Other that, when introjected, transforms into a tyrannical Master Signifier (S1). Being repeatedly named as "the incompetent," "the disappointment," "the sick one" is to be captured by a **Maledicta** word that petrifies identity and condemns to the repetition of a destiny. It is the alienation of Chapter 1 taken to its perverse paroxysm.

3.4.1 The Discourse of the Master and the Injunction as a Violent Speech Act

This violence is structured in the **Discourse of the Master**, where the signifier of the Master (S1) dominates knowledge (S2) and reduces the subject ($) to the condition of a disposable object (a). The word, in this discourse, does not aim at truth or the production of subjectivity, but at the maintenance of power and the reproduction of an order that crushes desire. The insult is the speech act that materializes this discourse in the social bond, producing an effect of the Real on the body and psyche of the other. A teenager who is constantly called "stupid" by his parents may, over time, completely introject this signifier, becoming a student who does not allow himself to succeed, as that would go against the "truth" of the name imposed upon him. His anxiety attacks before exams are the body's response to this **Maledicta** word, a form of jouissance that confirms, through failure, the alienating identity.

The ethics of psychoanalysis rises as a response to this violence. It is a bet on the **Benedicta** word—not the word of the Master, but the full word of the subject—as a tool to dismantle the curse of the name and forge an identity that is not a mere repetition of the alienating verdict of the Other. The analytical work here would consist in helping this teenager detach himself from this imposed S1, to question this "truth" and find his own words to name himself, transforming the **Maledictus** of the insult into a **Benedictus** of his own singular history.

3.5 The Indomitable Real and the Challenges of Cure

This chapter explored the radically constitutive limits of the word. If the word can cure (Benedictus), it also fails, petrifies, and wounds (Maledictus). Lalangue, the symptom as repetitive jouissance, the unsayable trauma, and the violence of the name are the manifestations of a Real that resists symbolization.

Through clinical examples—the migraine anchored in the materiality of the word, the repetition of failed relationships, violence as passage à l'acte, and the introjected insult—it was possible to gauge the concrete texture of this Maledictus. This exploration does not represent pessimism, but necessary clinical realism.

Recognizing the Maledictus is recognizing that the cure does not consist in saying everything—for the everything is not sayable—but in inventing a new relationship with this indomitable remainder. The next moment of investigation will demand examining the role of the analyst and the status of his word: how to operate precisely at the limit between the Benedictus and the Maledictus to provoke the emergence of the subject? How to intervene when the word fails, and how to use this very failure as a lever for cure?

References

- FREUD, S. (1920). *Beyond the Pleasure Principle*. Standard Edition, vol. XVIII.
- LACAN, J. (1985). *The Seminar, Book XX: Encore*. New York: W.W. Norton & Company, 1998.
- LACAN, J. (1998). *Écrits*. New York: W.W. Norton & Company, 2006.
- LACAN, J. (1985). *The Seminar, Book XI: The Four Fundamental Concepts of Psychoanalysis*. New York: W.W. Norton & Company, 1998.
- LACAN, J. (1999). *The Seminar, Book V: Formations of the Unconscious*. Cambridge: Polity Press, 2017.
- LACAN, J. (1992). *The Seminar, Book XVII: The Other Side of Psychoanalysis*. New York: W.W. Norton & Company, 2007.

CHAPTER 4: DISCOURSE ABOUT

The Attempt at Capture: The Discourse of the Master and the Objectification of the Subject

Facing the indomitable Real that resists symbolization —explored in the previous chapter through traumatic silence, the symptom as a petrified word, and the performative violence of language—the investigation now advances to the domain where these impasses are structured socially. From the clinical confrontation with the limits of the word, we transit to the analysis of the discursive formations that organize the social bond.

The concept of Discourse, formalized by Jacques Lacan in Seminar 17, *The Other Side of Psychoanalysis*, reveals itself as a crucial tool to decipher the mechanics of these structures and locate the points of escape where subjectivity can escape total capture (LACAN, 1992). The "Discourse About" thus configures itself as the systematic attempt of the Other to capture the subject ($), reducing it to a disposable object (a) or an item in a totalizing knowledge ($ S_2 $).

The central thesis guiding this stage of investigation maintains that, although these discourses aim implacably at domination and classification, the very structure of language—being inherently pierced, and the subject, radically divided—guarantees a constitutive failure that makes total capture impossible.

It is precisely in this structural fissure that the possibility of resistance lodges itself and from where the truth of the subject stubbornly erupts.

4.1 The Formalization of the Four Discourses: The Matrix of the Social Bond

Lacan proposes four fundamental discourses—of the **Master**, **University**, the **Hysteric**, and the **Analyst**—which represent the elementary and possible matrices of the social bond.

Far from being mere descriptive categories, each

discourse is a **formal and fixed structure** composed of four places and four terms that rotate among themselves in a precise sequence.

This mathematical device demonstrates, in an elegant and irrefutable way, the logical impossibility of a totalitarian and closed social order.

The four fixed places are:

1. **Agent:** The position from which the discourse is emitted, the instance that commands and initiates the relation.
2. **Other:** The position to which the discourse is directed, the receptor that is interpellated and must respond.
3. **Product:** The inevitable, and often undesired, result of the discursive operation.
4. **Truth:** The hidden, repressed foundation that silently sustains the entire discursive edifice.

The four circulating terms are:

1. S_1 **(Master-Signifier):** The signifier that commands without justification, the word that imposes an identity and does not articulate itself in a chain (the Father, the Boss, the Nation, Profit).

2. **$ S_2 $ (Knowledge):** The set of articulated signifiers, established knowledge, technique, bureaucracy, "know-how."

3. **$ (Barred Subject):** The subject of the unconscious, divided, the truth that escapes any total representation.

4. **a (object a):** The object cause of desire, the indomitable remainder, the plus-de-jouir that remains from every symbolic operation.

The base matrix, from which all other discourses derive by a quarter-turn counterclockwise, is that of the Discourse of the Master:

Discourse	Agent	Other	Product	Truth
Master	$ S_1 $	$ S_2 $	a	$
University	$ S_2 $	a	$ S_1 $	$
Hysteric	$	$ S_1 $	$ S_2 $	a
Analyst	a	$	$ S_1 $	$ S_2 $

This formal structure is not an abstract game. It demonstrates that no discourse can capture the totality of human experience. The impossibility of a total closure—what Lacan calls the "non-relation of the sexes"—resides in the very nature of language (incomplete) and the subject (divided), which are the $ and the *a* that always escape, always return as a disturbing real.

4.2 The Discourse of the Master: The Attempt at Domination and its Price

The Discourse of the Master is the **"Discourse About"** in its purest and most archaic form. In it, the Master-Signifier ($ S_1 $) arrogantly occupies the place of Agent, commanding Knowledge ($ S_2 $) which is in the subaltern position of Other.

$$ S_1 $ \rightarrow $ S_2 $$

....

$$ \rightarrow a$$

The Logic of Domination: In this structure, the Master (be it a tyrant, a patriarch, a capitalist imperative) imposes its law and its word without necessarily needing to justify it through coherent knowledge. It is the authority that is not discussed. The Other (the slave, the subject, the worker) is the one who must "know-how," execute, produce, translate the empty command into concrete action. The Master speaks; the slave works.

The Product and the Hidden Truth: The direct **product** of this operation is the object *a*, the plus-de-jouir extracted from the work and body of the slave, which sustains and feeds the jouissance of the Master. This is profit, surplus, the satisfaction of power. However, the hidden and repressed **truth** of this discourse is the Barred Subject ($) of the Master. To command, he needs to erase his own division, his own lack, his castration. He must present himself as complete, but his position is sustained by a truth of incompleteness.

This discourse is the formalization of the primordial alienation explored in Chapter 1 (**Maledictus**). The word here is profoundly **Maledicta** because it is the blind instrument of a domination that objectifies and exploits.

Expanded Clinical Example: Imagine a patient, a successful executive, who seeks analysis due to a panic crisis. He discovers that his entire life was oriented by an incontestable paternal mandate—"You must be a winner, an example for the family"—which functioned as a tyrannical $ S_1 $. His "know-how" ($ S_2 $) was impeccable: diplomas, strategies, networking. The **product** of his life was an anguished jouissance (a), a paradoxical satisfaction in the very exhaustion and empty recognition. The repressed **truth** ($) was his infantile desire to simply play, his real disinterest in the corporate race. Analysis, in this case, aims to make this truth emerge, dislodging him from the Discourse of the Master that had strangled him.

4.3 The University Discourse: Domination Dissimulated by Knowledge

The University Discourse is the modern, "enlightened," and dissimulated form of the Discourse of the Master. It is here that power becomes more insidious. In it, Knowledge ($ S_2 $) occupies the place of Agent, directing itself to the object *a* in the position of Other.

$ S_2 $ → a

....

$ ← $ S_1 $

The Logic of Objectification: Power no longer presents itself as the explicit command of a tyrant, but as the impersonal, cold, and supposedly neutral authority of objective knowledge, science, technique, protocols, and bureaucracy. The subject is treated not as a person, but as an object of study (a), a clinical case, a CPF number, a statistical datum, a human resource. The discourse does not say "obey me," but "this is a fact," "data shows," "the protocol demands."

The Perverse Product and the Denied Truth: The **product** of this discourse is, paradoxically, a new Master-Signifier ($ S_1 $). The supposedly neutral knowledge generates new tyrannical ideals: maximum efficiency, productivity, statistical normality, eternal youth. The **truth** that remains hidden and denied is, once again, the Barred Subject ($), whose singularity, history, and desire are crushed in the name of universal classification.

The word in this discourse is **Maledicta** for its claim to total neutrality and objectivity, which masks profound symbolic violence.

Expanded Clinical and Social Example:

- **In the Clinic:** A patient arrives at a public health service and is received not by an ear, but by a form. He is quickly categorized as "Borderline Personality Disorder, F60.3." This diagnosis ($ S_2 $) begins to command his entire treatment, reducing him to an object (a). The **product** is the crystallization of this master-signifier ("I *am* borderline") which imprisons his subjectivity. The **truth** of his singular suffering, his history of abandonment, his constitutive division ($), is obliterated by the classification.

- **In Society:** State bureaucracy, transforming citizens into numbers in a system, is another potent manifestation of this discourse. The algorithm of a social network that transforms desires and affects into marketable data (a) to produce the master-ideal ($ S_1 $) of perfect consumption is the University Discourse in its contemporary technological form.

4.4 Resistance: The Discourses of Subversion

The genius of Lacanian formalization is to show that the structure of discourses contains within itself the seeds of resistance. The truth of the subject ($) and the object *a* cannot be totally absorbed, and it is from this intrinsic failure that the discourses of subversion arise.

4.4.1 The Discourse of the Hysteric: The Tireless Interrogation that Generates Knowledge

In the Discourse of the Hysteric, the Barred Subject ($) finally assumes the position of Agent, directing itself directly to the Master-Signifier ($ S_1 $).

$$\$ \to \$ S\_1 \$$$

$$\ldots\ldots\ldots\ldots$$

$$a \leftarrow \$ S\_2 \$$$

The Logic of Questioning: The hysteric permanently puts the Master in check. Her suffering, her symptom (the object *a* in the place of Product) is a living, pulsating, and painful questioning directed at authority: "What do you want from me?", "Why am I like this?", "What is a woman?". She does not accommodate herself to the identity offered to her. By interrogating the $ S_1 $, she forces it to produce knowledge ($ S_2 $) to try to explain her, answer her, calm her. The hysteric is the engine of knowledge production in civilization, but no knowledge is ever sufficient to silence her fundamental question.

This discourse is a form of active and destabilizing resistance to being "spoken" by the Other. It is the refusal to accommodate oneself to a fixed identity, keeping alive the flame of interrogation about one's own desire. The word here is, at the same time, **Maledicta** in the suffering of the symptom and **Benedicta** in its infinite power of questioning.

4.4.2 The Discourse of the Analyst: The Ethics of the Emergence of the Subject

The Discourse of the Analyst is the direct antithesis of the Discourse of the Master and the royal road to analytic cure. In it, a Copernican revolution occurs: the analyst places himself in the place of Agent, but not as a master or a sage, but as **object *a***, directing himself to the Barred Subject ($) of the analysand.

a → $

....

$ S_1 $ ← $ S_2 $

The Logic of Analysis: This is the great ethical turn. The analyst is not the holder of knowledge ($ S_2 $) about the patient. He offers himself as object cause of desire, as an emptiness, an opaque presence that provokes the subject to speak, to associate freely, and to confront its own constitutive division ($). The analyst "does not know," he listens. His silence and his punctual interventions (cuts, punctuations) aim to sustain this place of the object.

The Product of Cure: The **product** of this work is not adaptation, but the production of a new Master-Signifier ($ S_1 $). This is no longer a signifier imposed by the social or familial Other, but a singular signifier, proper to the subject, which emerges from its unconscious and allows it a new articulation of its desire. It is the word that, finally, represents it in a less alienating way. The **truth** that sustains and is revealed in this process is the Knowledge ($ S_2 $) of the unconscious, which is gradually constructed, deciphered, and, finally, appropriated by the analysand himself.

Here, in the Discourse of the Analyst, the word reaches its apex as **Benedicta**. This discourse is the materialization of the bet on the full word. It is not a "Discourse About" the subject, but a meticulously constructed device for the subject to speak *of* itself and, in doing so, emerge and assume itself in its constitutive division, inventing a new way of enjoying and inhabiting the world.

4.5 The Discursive Structure and its Ethical Impasses

The analysis of the Four Discourses demonstrated how the word, when organizing itself into social structures, can serve both the capture and objectification of the subject—becoming Maledicta in the discourses of the Master and the University—and its liberation and affirmation—becoming Benedicta in the discourses of the Hysteric and the Analyst. The Lacanian formalization reveals that totalitarian power is a structural impossibility, for the barred subject ($) and the object a constitute an irreducible remainder, a "not-all" that always escapes domination and disturbs the established order.

Resistance thus shows itself not as an accident or moral virtue, but as a necessary consequence of the structure of language and subjectivity. The psychoanalytic clinic is founded precisely on the ethical bet of the Discourse of the Analyst, creating an artificial space where the "Discourse About" is systematically suspended to allow the subject to invent its own saying and forge its singular master-signifier.

This understanding of discursive structures prepares the ground for the ultimate investigation: ethics in its maximum radicality, where the act of the word transcends mere saying to convert itself into an ethical gesture of affirming desire beyond all symbolic captures. The next stage will examine this moment of passage to the act at the very core of language, where the invention of the subject reaches its most radical expression.

References

- LACAN, J. (1992). *The Seminar, Book XVII: The Other Side of Psychoanalysis*. New York: W.W. Norton & Company, 2007.

CHAPTER 5: DISCOURSE OF THE SUBJECT

*The Crack of Desire: The Emergence of
the Full Word and Unconscious Truth*

From the structural analysis of social discourses—which revealed both the mechanisms of capture of the subject and the inevitable fissures where resistance surges—now emerges the ethical heart of the psychoanalytic project. If the mapping of the discourses of the Master and University demonstrated the objectification of the subject, and the discourse of the Hysteric pointed to radical questioning, it is in the Discourse of the Analyst that we find the possibility of the emergence of the Discourse of the Subject.

This transition from the analysis of structures of capture to the emergence of authentic word represents the crucial turning point in the analytic journey. It is the moment when the word, previously Maledicta for its alienating function in the Discourse About, reveals itself fully as Benedicta as an instrument of liberation and affirmation of singular truth. We explore here the word that does not describe the subject from the outside, but constitutes it from its most intimate crack—the advent of the word that cures because it is true, and that is true because it engages desire at its most fundamental root.

5.1 The Full Word and the Empty Word: The Battlefield of Analysis

The foundation for understanding the Discourse of the Subject is the fundamental distinction, established by Lacan in *The Function and Field of Speech and Language*, between **empty speech** (*parole vide*) and **full speech** (*parole pleine*). This is not a mere classification, but the axis around which the direction of the treatment and its ethics revolve.

Empty speech is the discourse of the surface, of *chatter*. It is the speech that exhausts itself in instrumental communication, in the repetition of social and familial clichés, and in the defense of the imaginary ego. In it, the subject speaks *about* itself, but does not speak *from* itself. It is the realm of the internalized

"Discourse About," where the subject repeats the master-signifiers ($ S_1 $) of the Other without subjectively implicating itself. Lacan (1998, p. 256) describes it as a "repetition without meaning," a discourse that, although it may be coherent and factually accurate, is empty of subjective truth because it does not touch unconscious desire. A patient who meticulously reports the events of his week, but does so in a dissociated manner, as if narrating the life of a stranger, is delivering empty speech.

In radical opposition, **full speech** is the discourse that *makes an event*. It is not defined by content, but by its function of **activating subjective truth**. It is the word that, when articulated, resonates in the crack of the subject, revealing it to itself in a new and often surprising way. It does not "tell the truth," but *makes* the truth emerge. Lacan (1998, p. 256) affirms that it "constitutes the truth of the subject." This word has the power to resignify the past (*après-coup*) and open a different future. It occurs in the instant of the slip, in the affect that breaks the controlled narrative, in the sudden memory that connects dispersed symptoms.

The analyst's work is, precisely, to create the conditions for this crossing. Through silence, punctuation, and the cut, the analyst interrupts the flow of empty speech, introducing fissures where full speech can erupt. Analysis is, in its central operation, a long and patient battle for the passage from one modality of speech to the other.

5.2 The Discourse of the Subject: The Assumption of the Desiring Crack

The **Discourse of the Subject** is the existential and discursive field where full speech becomes possible. It rises upon the recognition and assumption of two fundamental truths: the **crack of the subject** ($) and the primacy of **desire**.

The **crack** is the indelible mark of the human being's entry into language. The subject is barred ($) because it is an effect of the signifier, but can never be totally represented by it. There is always a remainder, an irreducible division between the subject of the enunciation (who speaks) and the subject of the statement (the "I" of whom is spoken). The Discourse of the Subject is one that does not try to artificially suture this crack with the imaginary identifications of the ego, but assumes it as the condition of its existence. It is a discourse that accepts incompleteness.

Desire, the other pillar, is understood here not as a biological drive, but as the metonymic engine of subjectivity. Following the Lacanian formula (Desire = Demand - Need), desire is what escapes the duality need/demand. It is the very mobility of lack, which slides incessantly in the signifying chain. The Discourse of the Subject is one that orients itself by this lack, that lets itself be guided by desire, instead of trying to fill it with the consumption objects the Other offers.

Crucially, the emergence of this discourse depends on the unveiling of a third truth: the **incompleteness of the Other** (A). The alienated subject lives under the illusion that the Other (parents, society, partner) holds the key to its being and completeness. The Discourse of the

Subject is born from the collapse of this illusion. Upon perceiving that the Other is also barred, pierced, and does not possess the object that would complete it, the subject can finally "separate" and assume responsibility for its own desire and its own lack.

5.3 The Subject of the Unconscious ($) and its Formations

The agent of the Discourse of the Subject is the **Subject of the Unconscious** ($). This is not the conscious ego, but the subject of division, which manifests itself in moments of rupture of conscious discourse. Its appearance is the materialization of full speech. Lacan, returning to Freud, locates its theater of operations in precise formations:

1. **The Parapraxis (*Fehlleistungen*):** The slip, forgetting a name, a stumble of the tongue. These are not errors, but *successful actions of the unconscious*. A man who, when speaking of his wife, calls her by his ex-partner's name is not "erring"; he is, through his unconscious, enunciating a truth about his libidinal economy that his conscious discourse would want to silence. The parapraxis is the tip of the iceberg of desire erupting onto the policed surface of empty speech.

2. **The Dream:** The "royal road to the unconscious." The dream is the Discourse of the Subject in a pure

state, during sleep. Through condensation (one signifier represents several others) and displacement (affect displaces to an apparently insignificant element), the dream ciphers desire. Working a dream in analysis is not "deciphering it" to find a hidden meaning, but exploring its signifying connections so that the analysand can, itself, be surprised by the truth its own mind produced.

3. **The Joke (*Witz*):** The formation of the unconscious that provokes laughter. The joke operates through an economy of psychic energy: it bypasses censorship and allows the expression of an aggressive or sexual thought in a socially acceptable form. The pleasure of the joke comes from this sudden release, from the eruption of desire into the field of the Other in a successful and shared way.

Analytic interpretation, far from being the application of a prior knowledge of the analyst, is the art of **punctuating** these formations. It is to isolate a signifier from the dream, repeat the slip, or explore the logic of the joke, so that the analysand itself is confronted with the enunciation of its unconscious. Interpretation aims to produce a "subject effect," forcing it to recognize itself in that which it itself said without knowing.

5.4 The Ethics of Psychoanalysis: The Commitment to Well-Saying

The culmination of the Discourse of the Subject is of an ethical order. The ethics of psychoanalysis, as formulated by Lacan, is not a social morality. It is an ethics of **well-saying** (*bien-dire*) and **not giving ground relative to one's desire** (*ne pas céder sur son désir*).

Well-saying is not empty eloquence. It is the courage to sustain the full word, to continue speaking even when the emerging truth is painful, embarrassing, or goes against the expectations of the "Discourse About." It is the commitment to seek, incessantly, the words that best capture the truth of one's own desire, however provisional they may be.

Not giving ground relative to one's desire is the central ethical imperative. To "give ground" does not mean not to satisfy desire; it means *to betray it*, deny it, substitute it with the pursuit of objects the Other values (success, wealth, recognition) to the detriment of what is singular to the subject. It is what happens when someone abandons an artistic vocation to follow a bureaucratic career to please the family. Analysis aims to lead the subject to this point of choice: to give in to the desire of the Other or to affirm its own.

This ethical commitment translates into **subjective responsibility**. From the psychoanalytic perspective, the subject is responsible not only for its conscious acts, but also for its unconscious, its dreams, its slips. To assume the Discourse of the Subject is to assume responsibility for that which inhabits us, even without our conscious consent. It is to cease placing oneself as a victim of fate, parents, or society, and to recognize oneself as the protagonist—albeit divided and decentralized—of one's own history.

The end of a successful analysis is not happiness or adaptation, but the **traversal of the fantasy**. It is the moment when the subject unveils the fundamental structure that organized its relation with desire and can, then, detach itself from it. It is no longer about seeking the object that supposedly would complete it (the *object a* in the fantasy), but about assuming lack as constitutive and inventing, from it, a new way of living and enjoying. The Discourse of the Subject is, ultimately, the discourse of this conquered freedom: the freedom of a subject who, knowing itself divided and flawed, can finally "take its street band to the street" and affirm its singular desire in the world.

5.5 The Emergence of the Subject and the Passage to the Ethical Act

The articulation between the "Discourse About" and the "Discourse of the Subject" established the conditions of possibility for the emergence of the subject of the unconscious through the full word. It was demonstrated how the distinction between empty and full speech, articulated with the formations of the unconscious and the ethics of well-saying, allows the subject to transit from initial alienation to the assumption of desire.

The Discourse of the Subject thus revealed itself as the materialization of Benedictus at its maximum potency: the word that, when assumed in its truth, operates subjective transformation and cure. This full word constitutes itself as an antidote to the Maledicta word of alienation and an instrument for the invention of an authentic existence.

In the next chapter, "The Act of the Word: The Ethics of Doing," the necessary unfolding of this discursive conquest will be examined. If the full word cures and transforms, the Act of the Word founds and institutes. The passage from the discursive recognition of the truth of desire to its ethical realization in action will be addressed—the decisive moment when speech converts into a foundational act of a new subjective position, constituting the ethical subject beyond all discursive mediations.

References

- FREUD, S. (1900). *The Interpretation of Dreams*. Standard Edition, vol. IV and V.
- LACAN, J. (1953). *The Function and Field of Speech and Language in Psychoanalysis*. In: Écrits. New York: W.W. Norton & Company, 2006.
- LACAN, J. (1964). *The Seminar, Book XI: The Four Fundamental Concepts of Psychoanalysis*. New York: W.W. Norton & Company, 1998.

CHAPTER 6: THE ACT OF THE WORD

The Ethics of Doing: From Alienation to the Assumption of Desire

The path that established the conditions for the emergence of the subject through the full word now finds its necessary ethical unfolding. If the previous chapter consolidated the possibility of the Discourse of the Subject as an antidote to alienation, this chapter examines the crucial moment when this saying converts into a transformative doing.

The Act of the Word configures itself not as an external dramatic event, but as an internal transformation where the word, invested by the force of the drive, definitively breaks with the paralysis of the Discourse About and instates a new relation of the subject with its desire. This fundamental passage—from alienated complaint to desiring responsibility—represents the ultimate ethical horizon of the analytic experience, where the word reaches its maximum potency as an instrument of subjective foundation.

6.1 The Drive and the Word: The Energy that Moves Transformation

To understand the transformative force of the Act of the Word, it is necessary to resort to the concept of the **drive** (*Trieb*). In Freud, the drive represents the frontier between the somatic and the psychic; in Lacan, it articulates directly with the structure of language. The drive is not a raw biological impulse, but an assembly that circumscribes the **object a**—this remainder of jouissance that escapes symbolization—at the edges of the body.

The **death drive**, in particular, assumes a crucial role. Far from being only a destructive tendency, it is, for Lacan, the face of the Real that insists beyond the pleasure principle, manifesting itself both in the compulsion to repeat and in the possibility of its rupture.

The word, in its attempt to symbolize this drive-based Real, always partially fails. However, it is precisely in this failure, in this hiatus between the symbolic and the real, that the possibility of the Act opens.

The relationship between drive and word is, therefore, paradoxical. If the word "kills the thing" by symbolizing it (LACAN, 1998), the drive is what insists as a living and indomitable remainder. The Act of the Word occurs when the word no longer tries to completely domesticate the drive, but lets itself be **invested** by its energy, becoming the vehicle of a truth that breaks with the shackles of repetition. It is the drive, detached from the deadly circuit of the symptom, that confers upon the Full Word the necessary force to become a transformative Act.

6.2 The Psychoanalytic Act: Beyond Saying, a Doing

The **Psychoanalytic Act** is a precise technical concept in Lacan, which must be rigorously distinguished from other modalities of action, such as *acting out* and *passage to the act*. While the latter represent impasses in the relation with the Other, the Psychoanalytic Act is a symbolic operation that founds a new subjective position.

Concept	Register	Relation with the Other	Subjective Effect

Psychoanalytic Act	Symbolic	Breaks with dependence	Change of position (**Benedictus**)
Acting Out	Imaginary	Desperate appeal	Repetition (**Maledictus**)
Passage to the Act	Real	Traumatic rupture	Exclusion from the scene

The Psychoanalytic Act is, par excellence, an **act of the word**. It is not a "doing" in the external world, but a saying that, by its truth and timing, operates as a doing in the psyche. It is the moment when an interpretation from the analyst, or an association from the analysand, is not only comprehended, but **acted out** subjectively.

This act is not deliberate by the ego; it *befalls* the subject from its unconscious, as a certainty that imposes itself and reorganizes its libidinal economy.

The essence of the Act resides in **authorization**. The subject who acts no longer waits for permission from the Other (parents, society, superego).

It authorizes itself, from its own desire and constitutive division ($), to break with an alienating identification ($ S_1 $) and to assume a new form of existing. It is the passage from a position of object of the discourse of the Other to that of subject of its own desire.

6.3 The Passage of Position: The Temporal Logic of the Act

The Act of the Word obeys a specific **temporal logic**, which Lacan develops in "Logical Time." It does not occur in chronological and linear time, but in a logical time composed of three moments:

1. **The Instant of Seeing:** The subject is confronted with the evidence of its alienation. It is the moment of "There are those who say," where it perceives itself a prisoner of an alien narrative.

2. **The Time for Understanding:** Corresponds to the analytical work proper. The subject elaborates its stories, deciphers its symptoms, and, gradually, the truth of its desire becomes visible.

3. **The Moment of Concluding:** This is the instant of the **Act**. It is a leap, a decision under subjective urgency where the subject "concludes" that it can no longer remain in the previous position. It is not an intellectual conclusion, but a certainty that imposes itself and leads to an effective change.

This "moment of concluding" is the heart of the Act of

the Word. It is when the subject, for example, after years of analysis understanding its submission to a paternal mandate, says a simple phrase—"Enough!"—which is not a complaint, but a verdict that, upon being pronounced, dissolves an identification. The saying *is* the doing. The word, here, does not communicate; it acts.

6.4 Subjective Responsibility: The End of Excuse

The most radical effect of the Act of the Word is the instauration of an irreducible **subjective responsibility**. While the alienated subject lives in the realm of **excuse**—"I am like this because my parents made me like this," "Society oppresses me," "My boss doesn't value me"—the subject of the Act assumes that, no matter the past determinations, it is it who, in the present, sustains (or not) its position.

Assuming responsibility does not mean blaming oneself. It means recognizing oneself as the only agent capable of responding (*response-ability*) for its mode of jouissance and its choices, even the unconscious ones. It is the end of the position of victim of fate or the Other. The Act of the Word is, therefore, the materialization of **psychoanalytic ethics**: not giving ground relative to one's desire. To "give ground" is not to stop satisfying it, but to betray it, deny it in favor of the demand of the Other. The Act is the contrary affirmation: the courage to sustain one's own desire, with all the consequences that entails.

This assumption is intrinsically linked to the **fall of the Subject Supposed to Know**. The Act is only possible when the analysand perceives that the analyst does not hold the key to its desire. The knowledge that matters is in its own unconscious. The Act of the Word is, thus, the gesture by which the subject separates from the transferential dependence and "authorizes" itself from its own symptom and desire.

6.5 The Act and the Invention of the Sinthome

In his last teaching, Lacan speaks of the **sinthome** as the singular invention that each subject elaborates to make a bond with the Real of its jouissance. The Act of the Word can be understood as the moment of crystallization of a new sinthome—no longer the symptom as suffering (**Maledictus**), but as a creative and singular solution

(**Benedictus**).

An artist who, after years of block, finds his own style; a patient who transforms his anguish into a life project; someone who decides to radically change his career not out of escape, but out of alignment with a long-denied desire —all are examples of how the Act of the Word (which can be an internal act of decision, not necessarily an external deed) allows the subject to "sew" the three registers (Real, Symbolic, Imaginary) in a new way, inventing a form of living that is its own.

The Act, therefore, is not the end of analysis in the sense of a "cure" that erases division. It is, rather, the moment when the subject fully accepts being a **parlêtre**—a speaking and desiring being—and assumes the continuous task of inventing its life from this condition, without the crutch of the guarantees of the Other.

6.5 The Ethical Act and its Bodily Resonances

The present Chapter articulated the Act of the Word as

the culminating point of the analytic experience, where the Benedictus/Maledictus dialectic finds its ethical resolution: the word, once an instrument of alienation, converts itself into a vehicle of subjective liberation. Through the articulation between drive and symbolization, the distinction between the Act and its pathological forms, and the analysis of the inherent temporality and responsibility, it was demonstrated how psychoanalysis conceives the possibility of real subjective change.

The Act revealed itself not as a miracle, but as a possible consequence of a long work of speech, which culminates in the instant when the subject authorizes itself to exist from its own desire. This conquest, however, does not exhaust itself in the symbolic register, demanding to be investigated in its bodily manifestations.

In the next chapter, "The Word and the Body," it will be examined how this ethical act resonates in the organism, transforming it into a speaking body (parlêtre). The inscription of jouissance and the mark of the said in the flesh will be explored, where the word not only signifies, but literally inscribes itself, constituting a body that enjoys in a singular way.

References

- LACAN, J. (1964). *The Seminar, Book XI: The Four Fundamental Concepts of Psychoanalysis*. New York: W.W. Norton & Company, 1998.
- LACAN, J. (1998). *The Function and Field of Speech and Language in Psychoanalysis*. In: Écrits. New York: W.W. Norton & Company, 2006.
- LACAN, J. (2005). *The Seminar, Book XXIII: The Sinthome*. Cambridge: Polity Press, 2016.

CHAPTER 7: THE WORD AND THE BODY

The Speaking Body (parlêtre):
The Inscription of Jouissance
and the Mark of the Said

The realization of the Act of the Word as an ethical gesture of subjective liberation leads inevitably to the question of its bodily manifestations. If the act instates a new desiring position in the symbolic register, it is in the body that this transformation finds its ultimate materiality and its most tangible marks.

This chapter advances in the exploration of the parlêtre—the speaking being—as an entity indelibly marked by language. We will investigate how the word, far from being only representation, inscribes itself literally in the flesh, constituting a body that enjoys in a singular way. The analysis will focus on the inscription of jouissance and the mark of the said, where the symbolic and the real interlace in a radical way, revealing the limits and possibilities of psychoanalytic cure in facing the unsayable that inhabits the organism.

Here, the Benedictus/Maledictus dialectic reaches its most crucial point: if the word can cure and symbolize, it also necessarily fails before the real of the body, leaving a remainder of jouissance that resists all signification. It is on this frontier between the sayable and the unsayable that the ultimate possibility of a cure is played out, a cure that does not deny the real but invents new ways of dealing with it.

7.1 The Parlêtre: The Body that Is Language

The concept of **parlêtre**, central in Lacan's last teaching, represents a crucial displacement in relation to the classical notion of "subject." While the subject ($) was an effect of the symbolic structure, the parlêtre is the **being of jouissance** that results from the incidence of language on the biological body. The parlêtre does not *have* a body; it *is* a speaking body.

Entry into language is an event of **separation and**

marking. The biological organism, governed by need, is intercepted by the symbolic network of the Other. The primordial signifiers—the name, the familial master-signifiers ($ S_1 $)—inscribe themselves on the body as real marks, creating what Lacan calls the "speaking body." This inscription is not metaphorical; it is a real process that transforms the drive-based economy of the organism, creating zones of jouissance, fixations, and aversions that are absolutely singular for each parlêtre.

The body, therefore, is not a natural given, but a construction. It is the result of the "catching" of the organism by the symbolic. This is why there is no sexual relation that can be written in a universal formula: each parlêtre invents, through its unconscious, a singular way of making a bond with the other from its body marked by language.

7.2 Jouissance: The Real that Insists in the Body

To understand the relation between word and body, the concept of **jouissance** is essential. Jouissance is not pleasure. It is a satisfaction that goes beyond the pleasure principle, often paradoxical and linked to repetition and suffering. It is the **Real of the drive** that language cannot completely symbolize.

When the word "kills the thing" by symbolizing it, a remainder of jouissance always escapes. This remainder insists and returns, and its privileged place of return is the **body**. Jouissance is, therefore, what of bodily experience resists integral translation into words. It is the nucleus of opacity and repetition that sustains the symptom.

The notion of **plus-de-jouir** (surplus-jouissance) illustrates this economically. In Marx's wake, Lacan sees jouissance as a surplus, a "plus" that is produced by the very functioning of language. The parlêtre is one who produces and is harassed by this plus-de-jouir, incessantly seeking a complete satisfaction that the symbolic structure, being made of lack, makes impossible. This search is the engine of repetition and symptomatic suffering.

7.3 The Bodily Symptom: Between Conversion and Somatization

The body speaks. But it does so in two radically different ways, which demand distinct clinical interventions.

Hysterical conversion is paradigmatic of neurosis. An unconscious psychic conflict, unable to be represented, "converts" into a bodily symptom. A paralysis, blindness, a pain without organic cause are **bodily metaphors**. They have a meaning that can be interpreted and reinserted into the associative chain. Analysis seeks to transform this **Maledicta** word petrified in the body back into **Benedicta** word articulated in discourse.

Somatization (or the psychosomatic phenomenon) is of another order. Here, there is no metaphor. There is a **desertion of the subject** ($) from its position in the symbolic. The body does not "speak" a conflict; it is invaded by jouissance directly, without the mediation of the unconscious. Diseases like ulcers, certain dermatitis, or even autoimmune conditions can, in some cases, be readings where the Real of jouissance erupts without the protection of fantasy. Analytic intervention here is not to interpret a meaning, but to help the subject reconstruct a fiction (a fantasy) that can again mediate its relation with jouissance, "respiritualizing" the body invaded by the real.

Phenomenon	Register	Structure	Possibility of Interpretation
Hysterical Conversion	Symbolic	Metaphor (Signifier that substitutes another)	High (It is the **Maledicta** word that becomes body)
Somatization (Psychosomatic)	Real	Failure of metaphor, Jouissance without mediation	Low/None (It is pure jouissance, outside the chain)

7.4 The Inscription of the Word: The Sinthome as a Singular Solution

In his last phase, Lacan develops the concept of the **sinthome** to name the unique way each parlêtre "sews" or makes a bond between the three registers (Real, Symbolic, Imaginary). The sinthome is not only the symptom as suffering, but as a **life solution**, however dysfunctional it may seem.

The sinthome is the crystallization of a singular mode of jouissance. It is what allows the parlêtre to stabilize itself, albeit symptomatically. The work of analysis, in its final phase, is not necessarily to "cure" the sinthome, but to allow the analysand to **remake** or **assume it in a new way**. It is about transforming a **Maledictus** sinthome (source of suffering and repetition) into a **Benedictus** sinthome— a creative invention that organizes jouissance in a less pathological way.

An artist who transforms his anguish into a work; a craftsman who finds in the rhythm of his work a way to calm his restlessness; someone who discovers a passion that structures his time—all are examples of how a mode of jouissance can be resignified and become the axis of a livable life.

7.5 The Analyst's Word and its Effect on the Body

How can the analyst's word, which is pure signifier, have an effect on the jouissant body of the parlêtre? This is one of the most delicate questions of the clinic.

The analytic intervention does not act by suggestion or by a magical power of the word. It acts **structurally**.

By punctuating discourse, by making a cut, by isolating a signifier, the analyst provokes a **reorganization of the libidinal economy**. What was fixed and deadly jouissance in the bodily symptom can, through speech, be mobilized, displaced, and, eventually, reinvested in another form.

The **cut of the session** is a paradigmatic example. By interrupting discourse at the right moment, the analyst produces a lack. This lack, introduced into the symbolic, has a real effect on the body: it interrupts the jouissance saturation and opens a space for desire. The analyst's word, thus, does not "cure" the body directly, but modifies the **subjective position in relation to jouissance**, and it is this change that can have profound bodily effects.

The **analyst's desire**, manifested through his listening and interventions, is oriented towards a single goal: that the analysand can, by itself, reinvent its relation with the jouissance that inhabits it, finding for its sinthome a form that allows it to live in a more full and less suffering way.

7.5 The Inscribed Body and the Temporality of the Subject

Chapter 7 demonstrated that the psychoanalytic clinic cannot be reduced to a "cure by the word" in the sense of a pure symbolic elucidation. It is, necessarily, a clinic of the speaking body, of the parlêtre. The great challenge showed itself to operate at the tense limit between the Benedictus (the word that symbolizes, historicizes, and liberates) and the Maledictus (the real, mute, and repetitive jouissance that insists in the body).

Analysis does not promise the eradication of jouissance, but the possibility that the subject invents, through its speech and its act, a new way of inhabiting its body and dealing with what, in it, resists all signification. This conquest of a new relation with the body, however, needs to be understood in its temporal dimension.

In the next chapter, "The Word and Time," it will be examined how this invention unfolds in time, exploring the relation between the word, the act, and the temporality of the subject. The subjective rectification that allows the subject to rewrite its past, assume its present, and project a future beyond the repetition of the symptom will be addressed.

References

- LACAN, J. (1975-1976). *The Seminar, Book XXIII: The Sinthome*. Cambridge: Polity Press, 2016.
- LACAN, J. (1964). *The Seminar, Book XI: The Four Fundamental Concepts of Psychoanalysis*. New York: W.W. Norton & Company, 1998.
- MILLER, J.-A. *Being and the One*. Course of the Lacanian Orientation, 2010-2011.

CHAPTER 8: THE WORD AND TIME

*Subjective Rectification: Retroaction
and the Logical Time of Analysis*

The investigation of the word, which traversed from alienation to the ethics of the act, now reaches its fundamental temporal dimension. If psychoanalysis is founded as a "cure by speech," it operates a revolution in the very experience of time. Linear and chronological *chronos*, measurable by the clock, gives way to subjective *kairos*—a time of urgency, decision, and resignification that is proper to the unconscious.

This chapter explores how the word, when articulated in the analytic setting, unfolds a singular temporality, allowing the subject to rewrite its past, assume its present, and project a future beyond repetition. Far from being a mere report of what was, the psychoanalytic word reveals itself as a powerful temporal operator that **rectifies** subjective history, transforming the **Maledicta** repetition of the symptom into a **Benedictus** project of desire.

8.1 Logical Time: The Architecture of Subjective Decision

The psychoanalytic conception of time radically distances itself from the notion of a continuous and progressive line. Jacques Lacan, in his text *Logical Time and the Assertion of Anticipated Certainty* (LACAN, 1998), formalizes this experience through the concept of **Logical Time**, illustrated by the famous sophism of the three prisoners. This is not a theory about duration (*durée*), but about the logical structure of any process of decision and subjectivation. The three moments—**Instant of Seeing, Time for Understanding, and Moment of Concluding**—are not sequential and watertight phases, but logical times that can overlap, resume, and rearticulate throughout the analytic process.

The **Instant of Seeing** constitutes the first time, that of the sudden flash where the subject is confronted with a fragment of its truth that until then remained hidden. It is not a matter of intellectual comprehension or conscious deduction, but of an **anticipated certainty** that imposes itself in an almost traumatic way. It is the moment when anxiety, as a signal of the Real, erupts, breaking the illusion of coherence sustained by the ego. In the clinic, this instant can manifest through a revealing linguistic slip, the abrupt perception of a destructive pattern repeating in one's relationships, or the disturbing encounter with a master-signifier ($ S_1 $) that defines it in an alienating way. It is a time of suspension and strangeness, where the flow of empty speech is interrupted and something of the **Maledicta** truth of the subject insinuates itself, demanding elaboration.

The **Time for Understanding** succeeds the instant of seeing as a necessary period of elaboration, meditation, and psychic work. It is the realm par excellence of **Free Association**, where the subject is invited to weave and reweave its history, seeking to articulate with words what was only glimpsed in the previous flash. This time is intrinsically dialectical and non-linear: the subject constantly oscillates between resistance and *insight*, between the defensive comfort of empty speech and the rupture moments of full speech. Freud (1914), in *Remembering, Repeating and Working-Through*, already pointed out that the work of psychic elaboration (*Durcharbeitung*) is what allows effective transformation. It is in this time that the illusion of a past as a factual and immutable given progressively dissolves. The subject understands, in the transference relationship, that its history is a narrative construction, a weaving made with the signifiers of the Other that can—and should—be undone and remade. This is the time of analytic patience, where the laborious transmutation of the **Maledictus** of repetitive suffering into the **Benedictus** of an assumed and resignified truth operates.

The **Moment of Concluding** represents the third logical time, that of decision under subjective urgency. This conclusion is not the result of deliberate reasoning or a conscious choice of the ego. On the contrary, it is an **act** that imposes itself on the subject from its unconscious, as a necessary logical conclusion that springs from the previous work. This moment is the heart of the **Act of the Word**, explored in Chapter 6. A patient who, after years of analysis understanding his submission to a paternal mandate, one day surprises himself by saying "no" to a family demand in a serene and irrevocable way, is living a "moment of concluding." The force of the act resides not primarily in the content of what is said, but in the **change of subjective position** that this performative enunciation instates. The saying *becomes* a doing that redefines the subject in the world.

8.2 Retroaction (Après-Coup): The Rewriting of the Past on the Stage of the Present

The concept of **retroaction** (*Nachträglichkeit* in Freud, *après-coup* in Lacan) is one of the pillars that sustain the psychoanalytic conception of temporality. Through it, it is understood that the past is not a collection of objective and fixed events, stored in a mnemonic archive, but a **dynamic and continuous construction** that redefines itself permanently from the coordinates of the present.

Freud discovered, in his studies on hysteria, that a childhood event, often of a sexual character, only acquires its full pathogenic value **afterwards**, in puberty or adult life, when it is reinterpreted in light of new signifiers and a new libidinal economy. What was initially inscribed in the psyche as an isolated signifier, devoid of full meaning or traumatic affective charge, can, years later, be retroactively invested with a devastating meaning. Analysis operates precisely in this temporal logic: by bringing to light new associations, unprecedented connections, and unexpected affects in the context of transference, it allows a **new writing** of the past. A paradigmatic clinical example: a man who suffers from an intense social phobia may, in the course of analysis, retroactively connect his terror of speaking in public to a childhood scene of humiliation at school. At the time, the scene was lived with shame, but only became structuring of a disabling symptom much later, when, in his first job, the signifiers "authority" and "judgment" reacquired an unbearable weight, retroactively conferring a new meaning to the old humiliation.

The **word** is, therefore, the instrument par excellence of retroaction. When the subject narrates a memory in the analytic setting, it is not simply reproducing a passive record of a fact. It is, in that very act of narrating, **resignifying it**. With each new association made, each new affect that emerges in the transferential relation with the analyst, the past is symbolically rewritten. What was experienced as **Maledictus**—a traumatic and immutable destiny, a chain of signifiers that imprisoned—can, through this work, become **Benedictus**:

an assumed, integrated history and, above all, endowed with a new meaning that frees it from its pathological fixation. This **subjective rectification** of the past, far from being a mere exercise in reinterpretation, has as its necessary and ethical counterpart the opening of a radically different future, no longer predetermined by repetition.

8.3 Temporality and Ethics: From Determinism to the Project of Desire

Analysis, therefore, is not an archaeology of the psyche aimed only at the past. The rectification of the past by the word has as its ethical horizon the **opening of a future** in which the subject ceases to conceive itself as the mere determined product of its history to rise as the agent of a **project of desire**.

While the alienated subject lives under the sign of psychic determinism—"I am like this because my parents made me like this," "my history condemns me"—the subject in analysis is led to assume that, regardless of the determinations and signifiers that constituted it, it is it who, in the present, sustains (or not) its subjective position. This assumption, painful and liberating, is the *sine qua non* condition for a future that is not the mere reproduction of the past to become possible. **Desire**, once assumed in its dimension of structuring lack, becomes the compass that orients the subject in its temporal crossing. It is no longer dragged passively by the **Maledicta** current of the repetition of symptomatic jouissance, but begins to orient itself by the **Benedicta** ethics of the lack that moves and sustains desire. Analysis does not promise a future of full satisfaction and perennial happiness—an illusion that would belong to the imaginary register—but the concrete possibility of a future in which the subject can sustain its desire and be responsible for its choices, including the unconscious ones.

8.4 The Stabilization of Meaning: Points de Capiton and the Function of the Analyst

In a symbolic universe where, as Lacan demonstrated, meaning incessantly slides under the chain of signifiers, an anchoring operation that allows a provisional stabilization of meaning is necessary. Lacan (1998) called this fundamental operation **point de capiton** (*quilting point*). It is the logical moment when a signifier "quilts" a meaning to it, functioning as a pivot that, provisionally, interrupts the infinite drift and fixes a signification.

In the clinic, the analyst's intervention—an interpretation, a punctuation, a cut—can function as a point de capiton. By isolating a particular signifier from the analysand's discourse and attributing to it a provisional and operative meaning, the analyst helps stabilize and reorganize the discursive field, allowing the subject to read its experience in a new way. It is crucial, however, that both the analyst and the analysand understand that these points de capiton are necessarily **provisional** and not dogmatic. They are scaffolds that allow construction, not definitive walls. The work of analysis, in its direction, is precisely to enable the analysand itself to create, recreate, and dissolve its own points de capiton, making it progressively less dependent on the master-signifiers ($ S_1 $) of the Other and more the author of its own sinthome.

The time of analysis is, ultimately, the time of **transference**. It is in the living and current relation with the analyst that the logical times and retroaction operations are re-enacted, here and now. The analyst, by sustaining the place of the Subject Supposed to Know, offers an **other time**, a protected and *sui generis* time, where the subject can revisit the minefields of its past without being immediately devastated by them, and where it can risk anticipating, in the security of the setting, a different future. The **end of analysis**, in this perspective, is itself a temporal question. It is reached when the subject fully assumes the authorship of its time—when it becomes capable of operating, alone, the necessary retroactions and of sustaining the ethics of its desire in the weaving of time, without the crutch of the transference relationship.

8.5 The Conquest of Time and the Transferential Field

Chapter 8 demonstrated that the psychoanalytic word is a temporal operator of extraordinary transformative power. Through the structure of Logical Time, the mechanism of Retroaction (après-coup), and the stabilizing function of Points de Capiton, the analytic clinic allows the subject to radically rewrite its relation with time.

The subject ceases to be the passive and determined effect of a past experienced as Maledictus to rise as the ethical agent of a history in constant and open resignification. The word, which once carried the weight of a traumatic and repetitive destiny, reveals itself fully as Benedicta in its function as a tool of temporal liberation, opening the concrete possibility of a future oriented not by the compulsion to repeat, but by the assumed and desiring lack-to-be. This temporal conquest, however, does not occur in a vacuum, but in the specific relational field of transference.

In the next chapter, "The Word and Transference," the relational field where this temporal transformation unfolds most crucially will be examined. Transference as the engine of analytic cure and the ethics of the analyst's desire as the condition for the subject to rewrite its history and assume its desire will be explored.

References

FREUD, S. (1914). *Remembering, Repeating and Working-Through.* Standard Edition, vol. XII.
LACAN, J. (1998). *Logical Time and the Assertion of Anticipated*

Certainty. In: **Écrits**. New York: W.W. Norton & Company, 2006.
LACAN, J. (1998). *The Function and Field of Speech and Language in Psychoanalysis*. In: **Écrits**. New York: W.W. Norton & Company, 2006.

CHAPTER 9: THE WORD AND TRANSFERENCE

*The Analytic Bond: The Analyst's Desire
and the Sustenance of Discourse*

If the word constitutes the instrument of psychoanalysis and time its matter, **transference** establishes itself as its fundamental engine and field of practical realization. Since its discovery by Freud, this phenomenon defines not a mere technical accessory, but the very condition of possibility of the analytic process.

This chapter investigates transference through the prism of the word, understanding it not as simple affective repetition, but as **living enactment of the discursive structure** of the subject. It is in the laboratory of the analytic relation that the **Maledicta** word of the compulsion to repeat can transmute into the **Benedicta** word of the desiring assumption, a process that depends intrinsically on the ethical position sustained by the **analyst's desire**.

9.1 Transference as Actualization of the Reality of the Unconscious

For Jacques Lacan, transference represents much more than the reedition of infantile relational models; it is the **very actualization of the reality of the unconscious** in the here-and-now of the cure (LACAN, 1988). It configures itself as a true *mise-en-scène* of the master signifiers (S_1) that organize the psychic economy of the subject. The patient, by directing its discourse to the analyst, is not simply relating its history; it is **enacting it** in the immediacy of the transferential bond.

In this psychic theater, the analyst is invested with a specific place in the analysand's drama. As Pissetta (2011) points out, he becomes the **Other** (A) to whom the word is directed, the depositary of the alienating signifiers of the **Discourse About** and the privileged interlocutor for the emergence of the **Discourse of the Subject**. A patient who persistently places himself in the position of "the one who is betrayed," for example, is not just describing experiences; he is *situating the analyst in the place of the traitor*, re-actualizing a master signifier like "trust is always broken." The word, in this context, is profoundly performative: it instates the psychic reality it names.

Positive transference, therefore, transcends the notion of a "good relationship." It is the successful installation of a setting where the subject can repeat, in a sufficiently contained way, the signifiers that imprison it, nourishing the hope (unconscious) of a different outcome. The analysand's word in transference is, by essence, a **directed and demanding word**. It awaits a response, a recognition, a confirmation—and it is in this expectation that the lever for clinical intervention resides.

9.2 Transference Love and the Function of the Subject Supposed to Know

Transference love constitutes the affective manifestation par excellence of this process. Freud already identified it as the greatest obstacle and, paradoxically, the most powerful lever of analysis. Lacan (1992) radicalizes this understanding in his Seminar 8: transference love is **love directed to knowledge**—more precisely, love for the **Subject Supposed to Know** (SSS).

The SSS is a **structuring function**, not an inherent quality of the analyst. It is the supposition, on the part of the analysand, that the analyst holds the key to its enigma, that he "knows" the ultimate meaning of its symptom and the truth of its desire. This supposition, as Torres (2016) discusses, is a "necessary deception" that instates the proper field of analysis. The patient loves in the analyst not the concrete person, but the knowledge attributed to him. It is a love directed to the signifier, not to the being.

This love is intrinsically ambivalent. On one hand, it motivates the analytic work: the patient speaks in expectation of finally being deciphered and recognized by the one who supposedly knows. On the other, it is an attempt to **suture the subjective division** ($). By loving the SSS, the subject seeks an imaginary completeness, an ideal that redeems it from its constitutive lack. The demand for love covers over the structure of desire.

The word, at the peak of transference love, becomes

particularly intricate. It presents itself as **full word**, impregnated with affect and conviction, but often operates as the most refined **empty word**, for it aims to capture the Other and obtain its confirmation, instead of aiming at the truth of desire. It falls to the analyst, as psychoanalytic ethics postulates, not to yield to this demand for love, sustaining the place of the SSS without identifying with it, so that transference love itself can become an object of analysis and reveal the desire underlying it.

9.3 Interpretation: Intervention in the Field of the Signifier

If the patient speaks from its signifying network, the primordial function of the analyst is to **interpret**. Psychoanalytic interpretation, in the Lacanian conception, is not a pedagogical explanation, a decoding of hidden meanings, or a veiled suggestion. It is, rather, a **precise intervention in the field of the signifier** that aims to produce an effect of subjective truth.

Authentic interpretation does not aim to be "correct" in a factual sense. Its goal is **clinical efficacy**. This efficacy resides in its capacity to **displace** the signifying chain petrified by the symptom, to introduce an equivocation, an ambiguity, a new possible meaning. As Dias (2019) discusses, Lacanian interpretation operates on the frontier between the signifier and the object, seeking to touch the real of jouissance. Lacan (1998), in his *Intervention on the Transference*, defines it as that act which "gives the signification of a symptom." It does not reveal a pre-existing secret, but **attributes a new signification** that allows the subject to reorder its experience in a novel way.

The privileged target of interpretation is the **master signifier** ($ S_1 $) that organizes the subject's jouissance. Isolating and operating on this signifier—for example, "sacrifice" for the obsessive, "unsatisfied desire" for the hysteric—proves more crucial than the reconstruction of infantile scenarios. Interpretation aims to reach the **Real** that insists in the repetition, not to symbolize it integrally (an impossible undertaking), but to allow the subject to establish a new relation with this indomitable remainder.

Interpretation often operates

through **punctuation** and the **cut**. A strategically placed silence, the emphatic repetition of a patient's word, ending the session at a point of anxiety—all constitute modalities of interpreting that, by interrupting the automatic discursive flow, force the subject to confront what was being enunciated. Interpretation, therefore, is not reduced to long expositions; it is, often, an act of **creative interruption** of conscious discourse to enable the irruption of the unconscious.

9.4 The Analyst's Desire: Ethics as Foundation

The invisible, yet absolutely fundamental, operator of this entire process is the **analyst's desire**. This is not a personal desire (like the desire to cure, to help, or to be loved), but a **structural ethical position**. It is a "pure desire," an obtuse desire that has as its sole object the **emergence of the Other's desire** (the analysand's).

The analyst's desire is what makes it possible for him to **sustain the place of object a** in the Analytic Discourse. The analyst does not place himself as a master who knows, a teacher who instructs, or a friend who advises. He offers himself as a **structuring void**, a lack-to-be, which functions as the cause of the analysand's desire. His discrete presence and his judgment-free listening create a hiatus, a permanent interrogation that incites the subject to question its own certainties and to formulate, autonomously, the question of its desire.

This is a counter-intuitive and ethically demanding position. It means abdicating the seductive power of being the SSS, of incarnating the loved ideal. It means accepting to be the representative of **symbolic castration**, the one who personifies the fact that the Other (the analyst) is also barred, also does not possess the lacking object. It is this renunciation that, paradoxically, generates the conditions for the analysand's **separation**. Upon perceiving that the analyst is not the one who will fill its lack, the subject is constrained to assume responsibility for its own desire and its own mode of jouissance.

The end of analysis, from this perspective, is marked by the **destitution of the Subject Supposed to Know**. Transference is not "dissolved" as if it disappeared, but is **resignified**. The analysand ceases to project onto the analyst the knowledge about its desire and assumes for itself the authorship of its symptom and existence. Transference love gives way not to indifference, but to a new type of bond, where the subject, having assumed its constitutive division, can finally dispense with the crutch of the Other supposed to know.

9.5 Transference and the Invention of the New

Chapter 9 demonstrated that transference is the dynamic nucleus of the analytic experience, the stage where the word reveals itself in its dual face of Maledictus and Benedictus. As an enactment of repetition, it is the terrain of old suffering; as the engine of cure, it is the vehicle of new truth. This delicate and potent process is sustained not by technical maneuvers, but by the radical ethics of the analyst's desire—a desire oriented not towards the patient's well-being, but towards the advent of its desiring truth.

This transferential crossing, however, finds its maximum realization in the subject's capacity to create something new from its own jouissance.

In the final chapter, "The Invention of the Word," the culmination of this path will be examined: the capacity of the subject to invent a new word, capable of naming, in a singular way, the unsayable of its jouissance and forging a new bond with the real. It will be explored how the subject, having traversed alienation and assumed its desire, can finally create its own master-signifier and invent a truly authorial existence.

References

DIAS, B. The logic of interpretation in Lacan: between the signifier and the object. Latin American Journal of Fundamental Psychopathology, v. 22, n. 1, p. 178-195, 2019.
LACAN, J. (1988). *The Seminar, Book 11: The Four Fundamental Concepts of Psychoanalysis*. New York: W.W. Norton & Company, 1998.
LACAN, J. (1992). *The Seminar, Book 8: Transference*. Cambridge: Polity Press, 2015.
LACAN, J. (1998). Intervention on the Transference. In: Écrits. New York: W.W. Norton & Company, 2006.
PISSETTA, M. A. A. de M. The subject supposed to know and transference. Ad Verbum, v. 6, n. 1, p. 87-102, 2011.
TORRES, R. Crucial problems for the formation of the analyst today: the subject supposed to know in question. Stylus, v. 32, n. 6, p. 45-58, 2016.

CHAPTER 10: THE INVENTION OF THE WORD

The Ethical Imperative: The Subversion of Discourses and the Creation of the Subject

This final chapter is the ethical culmination of the journey traveled. If the path began in the **fundamental alienation of the Discourse of the Other (Chapter 1)**, passed through the **Benedictus/Maledictus** dialectic of the symbolic function and the unsayable real, and was structured in the struggle between the **Discourse About** and the **emergence of the subject**, it now disembarks at the ultimate horizon of the analytic experience: the **Invention of the Word**. This is no longer the received, repeated, or deciphered word, but the created, singular word that subverts the established order and allows the subject to invent itself beyond the alienating dichotomy of "Blessed Cursed." It is about the ethical imperative of, having traversed fantasy, affirming one's own desire and assuming the authorship of an existence that, finally, belongs to it. It is the moment of "taking the street band to the street" not as an act of blind rebellion, but as an ethical gesture founded on the assumption of one's own lack.

10.1 The Poetic Word and the Creation of New Signifiers

Psychoanalysis, at its point of arrival, borders on poetry. Not by an aesthetic accident, but by a structural necessity. Jacques Lacan, in his last teaching, displaces the emphasis from language as a pure symbolic structure to the word in its creative and not-wholly-capturable-by-meaning function. The poetic word is, in this context, that which performs an active work on language, playing with the signifier to detach it from its consecrated meanings and, thus, create new senses. While common word repeats the already known ($ S_2 $), the poetic word erupts as a new singular Master-Signifier (S1), which names an experience hitherto unsayable.

This creation is the direct response to the failure of the Other (A barred). The subject, upon facing the incompleteness of the signifying treasure of the Other

—the realization that there is no signifier that totally represents it—is summoned to a singular solution. The poetic word is this response: the invention of a new signifier, even if provisional, that allows a new subjective tying. It is the passage from being an effect of the signifying chain to becoming, in act, its author. A patient who, after years trying to narrate an existential void, one day coins the expression "the whale hole" to describe it, is performing a poetic act. This singular signifier, "whale hole," was not in the dictionary of the Other; it was invented to give a form, albeit enigmatic, to the real of his jouissance. It ceases to be a mute symptom (Maledictus) and becomes a living metaphor (Benedictus) that organizes his experience.

This operation is what Lacan, in Seminar 23, will call *sinthome*. The sinthome is the singular and unanalyzable invention that each subject elaborates to make a bond with the real of its jouissance. While the symptom is deciphered in analysis, the sinthome is assumed and reinvented. The poetic word is, therefore, the proper activity of the sinthome: it is the continuous work of sewing the registers Real, Symbolic, and Imaginary through a signifying creation. The subject, by inventing its word, invents its own sinthome and, with it, the possibility of a more livable life. The poetic function of language reveals itself, thus, not as an ornament, but as the ethical dimension par excellence of the word, which allows the subject to subvert repetition and create a new reality for itself.

10.2 The Subversion of Established Discourses and Social Criticism

The invention of a singular word is not a private event. It has an inevitable consequence in the social bond: the subversion of established discourses. The subject who creates its own word necessarily breaks with the Discourse of the Master (Chapter 4), which operates precisely by imposing a universal Master-Signifier (S_1)—be it the Father, the Nation, the Market, or the Norm—that everyone must incorporate.

Lacanian theory of the four discourses provides the map of this subversion. The Discourse of the Master and the University Discourse are the social forms of the "Discourse About." They seek to capture the subject ($), reducing it to an object (a) or an item in a totalizing knowledge ($ S_2 $). The invention of the word, fruit of the Discourse of the Analyst, is an act of resistance to this capture. By creating a proper signifier, the subject displaces itself from a position of object of discourse to that of subject of desire. It no longer repeats the alienating verdict of the Other; it contests it with the force of its singular saying.

This subversion has an intrinsically **critical and political** effect. Psychoanalysis, by promoting the invention of the word, does not offer a political program, but generates a **political effect** from singularity. The subject who questions the master-signifier that defined it ("the failure," "the hysterical woman," "the productive worker") is, in the same act, questioning the social order that produces and sustains these categories. Its singular speech becomes living testimony to the bankruptcy of totalizing discourses.

A clinical example would elucidate this dynamic: a woman who, diagnosed as "borderline," introjected this master-signifier ($ S_1 $) as her ultimate truth. Her suffering was the Maledicta enactment of this label. The analytic work, instead of trying to "cure" her of borderline, aimed to lead her to invent her own words to name her pain, her history, and her desire. By doing so, she not only subverted the psychiatric discourse that objectified her, but also criticized, via the singular, a certain social logic that pathologizes and medicalizes malaise. The invention of the word is, therefore, an act of dealienation that reverberates in the social body, exposing its fissures and its incapacity to account for the real of each one.

10.3 The Invention of the Subject Beyond the "Blessed Cursed"

The invention of the word is, in its most radical consequence, the **invention of the subject**. What is invented, at the end of analysis, is not a new persona or an ideal ego, but the **subject of the unconscious** in its constitutive division ($), now assumed and no longer denied. This process, termed by Lacan the **traversal of the fantasy**, consists in the unveiling of the structure that organized the subject's relation with desire and the object *a*.

The fundamental fantasy ($ ◊ a) is the imaginary response the subject elaborated to the question of the desire of the Other. It is the secret script it repeats to try to obtain the impossible completeness. The "Blessed Cursed" is the very figure of this social fantasy: it is the subject who oscillates between glorification and condemnation, bound to an alienating identification that, even painful, confers a place upon it. Being the "cursed genius," the "black sheep," or the "savior of the homeland" are ways of existing under the sign of a master-signifier of the Other.

The invention of the subject occurs **beyond** this duality. By traversing the fantasy, the subject perceives that the object *a*—what it supposed would complete the Other and itself—is a mirage. It accepts that there is no final answer for its desire and that lack is structural. It is from this fundamental helplessness that invention becomes possible. It is no longer about being "blessed" or "cursed" in the eyes of the Other, but about **authorizing oneself** from one's own lack.

The invented subject is, therefore, one who creates

its **own mode of jouissance**. It is not "cured" of jouissance, but discovers a way to articulate it in a less suffering and more creative manner, through its sinthome. It is the subject who, like the artist, does not reproduce a model, but creates from its own psychic materials. The word, here, is the instrument of this creation. It no longer serves to demand the love of the Other or to confirm a pre-established identity. It serves to sustain desire and to name, each time, the singularity of an existence that affirms itself beyond any verdict.

10.4 The Final Invitation: The Ethical Imperative to Affirm One's Own Desire

The entire analytic path disembarks in a single **ethical imperative**, which is the intransigent nucleus of Lacanian psychoanalysis: **not to give ground relative to one's desire**. This imperative is not life advice or a morality, but a logical consequence of the structure of desire. To give ground relative to desire is not to stop satisfying it; it is **to betray it**, deny it in favor of the demand of the Other, to opt for the security of servitude to the detriment of the risk of freedom.

Lacan formulates this ethics as the ethics of **well-saying**. "Well-saying" is not speaking correctly or beautifully, but speaking from the place of the truth of desire, even—and especially—when this truth is painful, anguishing, and contrary to social expectations. It is the speech that assumes castration, that does not recoil before the real and that takes responsibility for what it says. The **Act of the Word (Chapter 6)** is the materialization of this well-saying: it is the moment when a saying, by its force of truth, operates a real change in subjective position.

The final invitation of this book is, therefore, a call to this ethical act. It is the invitation to **"take the street band to the street,"** as proclaimed in Sérgio Sampaio's song echoing since the Introduction. This metaphor does not mean an impulsive discharge, but the courage to definitively break with the **Discourse About**—with the ready-made narratives, the petrifying diagnoses, and the alienating identities—to affirm, with all consequences, one's own desire.

Taking the street band to the street is inventing one's

own word and, with it, one's own path. It is to assume the inevitable solitude of a desire that has no guarantees in the Other. It is to accept that the freedom conquered in analysis is not that of plenitude, but that of responsibility: the responsibility of being the author of one's symptom, one's jouissance, and one's history. The end of analysis is this point of departure: the subject, now agent of its desire, is summoned to invent, each day, the word that will allow it to dance with the real, without the crutch of the master crutches. The word, which once was the instrument of its curse, reveals itself, in the final act, as the blessed tool of its own invention.

10.5 The Invention of the Word and the Authorship of the Self

This Chapter established the Invention of the Word as the ethical horizon of psychoanalysis. The journey that began in the alienation of the Discourse of the Other culminates in the possibility of the subject creating, from its division and desire, a singular word that subverts the established order and invents a new way of existing.

The ethical imperative to affirm one's own desire configures itself as the ultimate invitation for the subject to assume the authorship of its life, becoming the artificer of its own sinthome. "Blessed Cursed: Discourse About and the Affirmation of the Subject" concludes with the certainty that the word represents the only path to freedom, but a freedom that demands the courage to invent, for itself, a new word capable of naming the unsayable of its jouissance and forging a new bond with the real.

This conquest of the authorial word, however, does not conclude in the analytic setting, but projects itself into existence as a whole.

References

- LACAN, J. (1975-1976). *The Seminar, Book XXIII: The Sinthome*. Cambridge: Polity Press, 2016.
- LACAN, J. (1969-1970). *The Seminar, Book XVII: The Other Side of Psychoanalysis*. New York: W.W. Norton & Company, 2007.
- LACAN, J. (1998). *The Function and Field of Speech and Language in Psychoanalysis*. In: **Écrits**. New York: W.W. Norton & Company, 2006.
- FIGUEIREDO, I. P. Truth and poetic interpretation in Lacanian psychoanalysis. *Latin American Journal of*

Fundamental Psychopathology, v. 21, n. 2, 2018.

- SEGANFREDO, G. C. The sinthomatic invention and savoir-y-faire. *Lacanian Psychoanalysis Association*, 2015.
- COUTO, L. F. S. Lacanian Discourses as Social Bonds. *Subjectivities Journal*, v. 18, n. 2, 2018.

CONCLUSION

At the end of this journey through the word—in its dual face of **Benedictus** and **Maledictus**—what reveals itself is the very cartography of human subjectivity as unveiled by psychoanalysis. We started from the fundamental observation that the subject emerges in and by language, but that this symbolic birth is, from the very beginning, marked by a constitutive alienation. The **Inaugural Word** of the Other, although **Benedicta** for inscribing us into the human order of culture and law, simultaneously shows itself **Maledicta** by capturing us in a network of alien signifiers, condemning us to repeat, initially, a destiny that was not chosen.

This dialectical tension between the blessing of symbolization and the curse of alienation showed itself to be the engine of the entire analytic process. We explored how the **Symbolic Function (Benedictus)** operates as a promise of cure, allowing the naming of lack, the inscription of desire, and the weaving of a singular history.

However, we inevitably encountered the limits of this operation: the **indomitable Real (Maledictus)**—traumatic silence, opaque jouissance, petrified symptom—persists as an irreducible remainder that the word never manages to fully apprehend.

The investigation of **Discourses** demonstrated how this tension is structured socially. The **Discourse About** —materialized in the Discourse of the Master and the University Discourse—is the incessant attempt of the Other to capture the subject, objectify it, and fix it in totalizing identities and knowledges. Against this petrification, rises the possibility of the **Discourse of the Subject**, which is not a ready discourse, but the emergence, through the **full word**, of the unconscious truth of the barred subject ($). It is in the crack of the parapraxis, the dream, and the joke that the subject of the unconscious irrupts, challenging the master narratives imposed upon it.

The apex of this crossing concretizes itself in the **Act of the Word**, the ethical moment when saying transforms into doing. Not an external doing, but an internal act of authorization where the subject, invested by the force of the drive, breaks with the position of object and assumes responsibility for its desire. This act, far from being an escape, is a deeper plunge into the very condition of **parlêtre**, the speaking being whose body is marked by jouissance and the letter. Analytic cure, thus, is not the elimination of suffering, but the invention of a new relation with one's own jouissance, the transformation of the **Maledictus sinthome** into a creative and singular solution—a **Benedictus sinthome**.

The **proper temporality of analysis**—with its logical times and the logic of retroaction (après-coup)—showed itself fundamental in this process. It allows the subject to rewrite its past, not to deny it, but to resignify it, releasing a future that is not the mere repetition of the same. And this entire path only becomes possible in the living field of **transference**, where the relation with the analyst—sustained by the **analyst's desire**—offers the stage for the enactment and, finally, the subversion of alienating master signifiers.

We conclude, therefore, at the horizon of the **Invention of the Word**. Psychoanalysis does not offer a final salvation, but an ethical imperative: **not to give ground relative to one's desire**. This means having the courage to "take the street band to the street," as proclaimed by the song echoing since the beginning—not as an act of blind rebellion, but as a gesture founded on the assumption of one's own lack. It is to invent, for oneself, a singular word capable of naming the unsayable of its jouissance and forging a new bond with the real.

Benedictus, Maledictus. The word that curses us is the same that redeems us. The one that alienates us in the Discourse of the Other is the one that liberates us in the emergence of the subject of the unconscious. The analytic path is precisely this crossing: the passage from the received, repeated, and alienating word to the created, invented, and proper word. A word that, by accepting its radical incompleteness, can finally become **Benedicta** for the subject who, having traversed fantasy, dares to affirm its desire and assume the authorship of its existence. This is the last word, which is not a closure, but a permanent invitation to the invention of the self.

APPENDIX: GLOSSARY OF KEY TERMS

1. FREE ASSOCIATION (FREUD)

"Fundamental method of psychoanalytic technique which consists in the patient expressing, without criticism or selection, everything that comes to mind" (FREUD, 1913, p. 135). "The fundamental rule is: communicate everything that passes through your mind, even if it seems unpleasant, ridiculous, trivial, or irrelevant" (FREUD, 1940, p. 33).

2. PSYCHOANALYTIC ACT (LACAN)

"The psychoanalytic act is not any act. It is an act defined by its structure, and this structure is that of the analytic discourse" (LACAN, 1967-1968). "That which introduces a modification in the subjective position of the subject" (LACAN, 1964, p. 50).

3. COMPULSION TO REPEAT (FREUD)

"Manifestation of the death drive by which the subject actively repeats, in a painful form, traumatic situations" (FREUD, 1920, p. 21). "The compulsion to repeat replaces the impulse to remember" (FREUD, 1914, p. 154).

4. ANALYST'S DESIRE (LACAN)

"The desire of the analyst is not a pure desire. It is the desire to obtain absolute difference, that which is produced when the subject finds itself faced with the alternative of its being" (LACAN, 1960-1961). "It is not the desire to cure, nor the desire to know, but the desire that the truth of the subject emerge" (LACAN, 1964, p. 233).

5. DISCOURSES (LACAN)

"The discourse of the master produces knowledge as its slave" (LACAN, 1969-1970, p. 31). "The discourse of the analyst is the reverse of the discourse of the master" (LACAN, 1969-1970, p. 51). "The discourse of the hysteric is that which interrogates the master" (LACAN, 1969-1970, p. 41). "The university discourse is that which reduces the subject to an object of knowledge" (LACAN, 1969-1970, p. 45).

6. JOUISSANCE (LACAN)

"Jouissance is what serves no purpose" (LACAN, 1972-1973, p. 11). "There is a satisfaction beyond

the pleasure principle" (LACAN, 1959-1960, p. 89).
"The symptom is the way each one enjoys the
unconscious" (LACAN, 1974-1975, p. 13).

7. BIG OTHER (LACAN)

"The Other is the place of the word" (LACAN, 1954-1955,
p. 267). "The unconscious is the discourse of the
Other" (LACAN, 1955, p. 16). "There is no Other of the
Other" (LACAN, 1957, p. 813).

8. UNCONSCIOUS (FREUD/LACAN)

"The unconscious is a system governed by specific laws,
among which the most important are condensation and
displacement" (FREUD, 1915, p. 187). "The unconscious is
structured like a language" (LACAN, 1957, p. 234).

9. LALANGUE (LACAN)

"Lalangue, is what speaks without knowing, and without
doubt, because of that, closer to the real" (LACAN,
1972-1973, p. 126). "Lalangue serves first to enjoy, to enjoy
its material" (LACAN, 1972-1973, p. 54).

10. SURPLUS VALUE (MARX)

"Surplus value is the difference between the value produced by labor and the wage paid to the worker" (MARX, 1867, p. 217). "Capital is dead labor which, vampire-like, lives only by sucking living labor" (MARX, 1867, p. 321).

11. PLUS-DE-JOUIR (LACAN)

"The plus-de-jouir is what is produced in the capitalist operation" (LACAN, 1969-1970, p. 80). "It is the object a raised to the power of the signifier" (LACAN, 1969-1970, p. 82).

12. NAME-OF-THE-FATHER (LACAN)

"The Name-of-the-Father is the signifier which, in the field of the Other, appears as the law" (LACAN, 1955-1956, p. 235). "The foreclosure of the Name-of-the-Father is what characterizes psychosis" (LACAN, 1955-1956, p. 277).

13. OBJECT a (LACAN)

"The object a is what falls from the subject in the operation of the constitution of the subject" (LACAN, 1964, p. 185). "It is the cause of desire" (LACAN, 1960-1961, p. 167).

14. FULL WORD AND EMPTY WORD (LACAN)

"The full word is that which aims at the realization of truth" (LACAN, 1953, p. 352). "The empty word is that which does not engage the subject" (LACAN, 1953, p. 351).

15. PARLÊTRE (LACAN)

"The parlêtre is the speaking being" (LACAN, 1975-1976, p. 13). "The unconscious is the fact that being, by the fact that it is speaking, is affected by the signifier" (LACAN, 1975-1976, p. 15).

16. PASSAGE TO THE ACT (LACAN)

"Passage to the act is an exit from the scene" (LACAN, 1962-1963, p. 152). "In passage to the act, the subject precipitates itself outside the field of the Other" (LACAN, 1962-1963, p. 154).

17. POINT DE CAPITON (LACAN)

"The point de capiton is the point by which the signifier quilts the signified" (LACAN, 1955-1956, p. 355). "It is the point of convergence that allows the temporary stabilization of meaning" (LACAN, 1955-1956, p. 356).

18. DRIVE (FREUD)

"Conceptual threshold between the psychic and the somatic" (FREUD, 1915, p. 122). "The partial drives seek to obtain pleasure from specific erogenous zones" (FREUD, 1905, p. 167).

19. REAL, SYMBOLIC, IMAGINARY (LACAN)

"The real is what always returns to the same place" (LACAN, 1954-1955, p. 49). "The symbolic is the world of the signifier" (LACAN, 1954-1955, p. 50). "The imaginary is the world of the image and identification" (LACAN, 1954-1955, p. 51).

20. SIGNIFIER (SAUSSURE/LACAN)

"The linguistic sign unites not a thing and a name, but a concept and an acoustic image" (SAUSSURE, 1916, p. 81). "A signifier is that which represents a subject for another signifier" (LACAN, 1957, p. 819).

21. SYMPTOM (FREUD/LACAN)

"Compromise formation between the repressed desire and the repressing forces" (FREUD, 1916-1917, p. 358). "The symptom is the way each one enjoys the unconscious" (LACAN, 1974-1975, p. 13).

22. SINTHOME (LACAN)

"The sinthome is what allows the subject to make a social bond" (LACAN, 1975-1976, p. 11). "The sinthome is what is most singular in the subject" (LACAN, 1975-1976, p. 13).

23. BARRED SUBJECT (LACAN)

"The subject is barred, divided by the signifier" (LACAN, 1957, p. 817). "The subject $ is the subject of the unconscious" (LACAN, 1964, p. 141).

24. SUBJECT SUPPOSED TO KNOW (LACAN)

"The subject supposed to know is he who is supposed to know what the unconscious is" (LACAN, 1964, p. 232). "It is the cornerstone of transference" (LACAN, 1964, p. 233).

25. TRANSFERENCE (FREUD/LACAN)

"New editions or replicas of the impulses and fantasies which must be awakened and made conscious" (FREUD, 1915, p. 445). "Transference is the actualization of the reality of the unconscious" (LACAN, 1964, p. 133).

26. TRAUMA (FREUD)

"Experience which, in a short space of time, increases the excitation in the psychic life so powerfully that its elaboration by the normal and habitual means fails" (FREUD, 1926, p. 90).

27. VERDRAENGUNG (REPRESSION) (FREUD)

"Repression is the fundamental concept of psychoanalysis" (FREUD, 1914, p. 16). "The essence of repression lies simply in turning something away, and keeping it at a distance, from the conscious" (FREUD, 1915, p. 147).

28. VORSTELLUNGSREPRÄSENTANZ (IDEATIONAL REPRESENTATIVE) (FREUD)

"The psychic representative of the drive" (FREUD, 1915, p. 122). "The unconscious representation is the thing-representation" (FREUD, 1915, p. 180).

BIBLIOGRAPHICAL REFERENCES

FREUD, S. (1905). *Three Essays on the Theory of Sexuality*. Standard Edition, vol. VII.

FREUD, S. (1913). *On Beginning the Treatment*. Standard Edition, vol. XII.

FREUD, S. (1914). *Remembering, Repeating and Working-Through*. Standard Edition, vol. XII.

FREUD, S. (1915). *The Unconscious*. Standard Edition, vol. XIV.

FREUD, S. (1916-1917). *Introductory Lectures on Psycho-Analysis*. Standard Edition, vol. XV-XVI.

FREUD, S. (1920). *Beyond the Pleasure Principle*. Standard Edition, vol. XVIII.

FREUD, S. (1926). *Inhibitions, Symptoms and Anxiety*. Standard Edition, vol. XX.

FREUD, S. (1940). *An Outline of Psycho-Analysis*. Standard Edition, vol. XXIII.

LACAN, J. (1953). *The Function and Field of Speech and Language in Psychoanalysis*. In: Écrits. New York: W.W. Norton & Company, 2006.

LACAN, J. (1954-1955). *The Seminar, Book 2: The Ego in*

Freud's Theory and in the Technique of Psychoanalysis. New York: W.W. Norton & Company, 1991.

LACAN, J. (1955-1956). *The Seminar, Book 3: The Psychoses*. New York: W.W. Norton & Company, 1997.

LACAN, J. (1957). *The Instance of the Letter in the Unconscious or Reason Since Freud*. In: Écrits. New York: W.W. Norton & Company, 2006.

LACAN, J. (1959-1960). *The Seminar, Book 7: The Ethics of Psychoanalysis*. New York: W.W. Norton & Company, 1997.

LACAN, J. (1960-1961). *The Seminar, Book 8: Transference*. Cambridge: Polity Press, 2015.

LACAN, J. (1962-1963). *The Seminar, Book 10: Anxiety*. Cambridge: Polity Press, 2014.

LACAN, J. (1964). *The Seminar, Book 11: The Four Fundamental Concepts of Psychoanalysis*. New York: W.W. Norton & Company, 1998.

LACAN, J. (1969-1970). *The Seminar, Book 17: The Other Side of Psychoanalysis*. New York: W.W. Norton & Company, 2007.

LACAN, J. (1972-1973). *The Seminar, Book 20: Encore*. New York: W.W. Norton & Company, 1998.

LACAN, J. (1974-1975). *The Seminar, Book 22: R.S.I.* (unpublished).

LACAN, J. (1975-1976). *The Seminar, Book 23: The Sinthome*.

Cambridge: Polity Press, 2016.

MARX, K. (1867). *Capital: A Critique of Political Economy*. Volume I. London: Penguin Classics, 1990.

SAUSSURE, F. (1916). *Course in General Linguistics*. New York: McGraw-Hill, 2011.

REFERENCES

CASTRO, J. C. L. de. The unconscious as language: from Freud to Lacan. **Casa**, v. 3, n. 1, 2009.

COUTO, L. F. S. Lacanian Discourses as Social Bonds. **Subjectivities Journal**, v. 18, n. 2, 2018.

DIAS, B. The logic of interpretation in Lacan: between the signifier and the object. **Latin American Journal of Fundamental Psychopathology**, v. 22, n. 1, p. 178-195, 2019.

FIGUEIREDO, I. P. Truth and poetic interpretation in Lacanian psychoanalysis. **Latin American Journal of Fundamental Psychopathology**, v. 21, n. 2, 2018.

FRANÇÓIA, Cristiane R. The Symbolic and the Psychoanalytic Clinic: The Beginning of Structuring. **Adverbum**, v. 2, n. 1, 2007.

FREUD, S. **Beyond the pleasure principle**. In: FREUD, S.

Standard Edition, vol. 18. London: Hogarth Press, 1955.

FREUD, S. **The interpretation of dreams**. In: FREUD, S. Standard Edition, vol. 4-5. London: Hogarth Press, 1953.

FREUD, S. **The unconscious**. In: FREUD, S. Standard Edition, vol. 14. London: Hogarth Press, 1957.

FREUD, S. **Remembering, repeating and working-through**. In: FREUD, S. Standard Edition, vol. 12. London: Hogarth Press, 1958.

FREUD, S.; BREUER, J. **Studies on hysteria**. In: FREUD, S. Standard Edition, vol. 2. London: Hogarth Press, 1955.

HEGEL, G. W. F. **Phenomenology of Spirit**. Oxford: Oxford University Press, 1977.

HEIDEGGER, M. **Being and Time**. New York: Harper & Row, 1962.

JOYCE, J. **Ulysses**. London: Penguin Classics, 2000.

LACAN, J. **Écrits**. New York: W.W. Norton & Company, 2006.

LACAN, J. **The Seminar, Book 2: The Ego in Freud's Theory and in the Technique of Psychoanalysis**. New York: W.W. Norton & Company, 1991.

LACAN, J. **The Seminar, Book 3: The Psychoses**. New York: W.W. Norton & Company, 1997.

LACAN, J. **The Seminar, Book 7: The Ethics of Psychoanalysis**. New York: W.W. Norton & Company, 1997.

LACAN, J. **The Seminar, Book 8: Transference**. Cambridge:

Polity Press, 2015.

LACAN, J. **The Seminar, Book 10: Anxiety**. Cambridge: Polity Press, 2014.

LACAN, J. **The Seminar, Book 11: The Four Fundamental Concepts of Psychoanalysis**. New York: W.W. Norton & Company, 1998.

LACAN, J. **The Seminar, Book 17: The Other Side of Psychoanalysis**. New York: W.W. Norton & Company, 2007.

LACAN, J. **The Seminar, Book 20: Encore**. New York: W.W. Norton & Company, 1998.

LACAN, J. **The Seminar, Book 23: The Sinthome**. Cambridge: Polity Press, 2016.

LUSTOZA, R. Z. The formation of the concept of the Name of the Father (1938-1958). **Ágora: Studies in Psychoanalytic Theory**, v. 21, n. 2, p. 235-249, 2018.

MARX, K. **Capital: A Critique of Political Economy**. Volume I. London: Penguin Classics, 1990.

MILLER, J.-A. The database of love. **Lacanian Option**, n. 28, 2000.

MILLER, J.-A. The six paradigms of jouissance. **Lacanian Option**, n. 26, 1999.

PISSETTA, M. A. A. de M. The subject supposed to know and transference. **Ad Verbum**, v. 6, n. 1, p. 87-102, 2011.

SAMPAIO, S. **I want to take my street band to the street**. Rio de Janeiro: CBS, 1973. 1 sound disc.

SAUSSURE, F. de. **Course in General Linguistics**. 27th ed. New York: McGraw-Hill, 2011.

SEGANFREDO, G. C. The sinthomatic invention and savoir-y-faire. **Lacanian Psychoanalysis Association**, 2015.

SHAKESPEARE, W. **Hamlet**. London: Penguin Classics, 2015.

TORRES, R. Crucial problems for the formation of the analyst today: the subject supposed to know in question. **Stylus**, v. 32, n. 6, p. 45-58, 2016.

ZANOLA, P. C. Alienation and separation in Lacan's Seminar 11. **Psychoanalytic Time**, v. 51, n. 2, 2019.

ZENONI, A. The course of Lacan's teaching on the question of the father. **Latin American Journal of Fundamental Psychopathology**, v. 10, n. 1, p. 11-23, 2007.

ABOUT THE AUTHOR

Elizeu Antônio De Assis

Mr. Assis is a psychologist and psychoanalyst. His initial training in Psychology was completed at Unicentro Newton Paiva (1992), followed by further studies at the Federal University of Ouro Preto (UFOP). He specializes in Child Psychology and holds a Master's degree in Communication, Information, and Health Sciences from the Oswaldo Cruz Foundation (FIOCRUZ/ICICT). Additionally, he earned a Ph.D. in History in 2020 from the Postgraduate Program in History (PPGHIS) at UFOP. Currently, he holds a tenured position at the State University of Minas Gerais (UEMG) and serves as a permanent faculty member at the Federal University of Ouro Preto (UFOP).